I0796064

THE BIBLE OF BRITISH TASTE

THE BIBLE OF BRITISH TASTE

STORIES OF HOME, PEOPLE & PLACE

RUTH GUILDING

DESIGN BY
JACK HENSHALL

FRANCES LINCOLN

Foreword

I recall, before I became friends with Ruth, spending hours trawling bibleofbritishtaste.com. I would finish a blog post and go back to the beginning, on a loop until I felt like I'd thoroughly drank everything in. It was, and still is, the best place to find the kind of houses I wanted to take a good nosy at. Seventeenth-century cottages, Cornish castles, weavers' houses in Spitalfields. The opposite of a glossy magazine stuffed with spotless kitchens and styled piles of unread coffee table books, her website celebrates homes that are lived in, in a way that is not glossy but vivid and real and intense, and belong to the kind of people that I want to know more about: potters and printmakers, gardeners and novelists.

And then there's all the delicious stuff inside these houses, hence the need to reread blog posts on a loop. Getting lost in a *Bible* article is akin to taking a proper house tour. The reader is treated to shots of patinated chair legs and exquisite cabinet detailing. Larder doors are flung open, books are taken off shelves and opened for us at the most interesting pages, plentiful close-ups of mantelpieces, fabric scraps, magazine cuttings and lunch preparations are provided.

As all of the people whose houses, studios, workshops and gardens are featured in this book will attest, Ruth definitely does not like things to be messed with before she rolls up in her Skoda estate. 'Don't tidy up.' This means that the images she captures on her trusty phone show things exactly as they are: blankets left half falling off beds and sofas, papers on desks and piles of clothes on floors. What you see is what you get, or rather what you get is what you see, and it feels as if I, as a reader, am not only being given a true and uncensored snapshot of a life, I am right there in the cottage/castle/caravan, perched on a chair arm and about to be handed a drink.

I've had the lucky opportunity over the past couple of years to assist in a small way with the creation of her *Bible of British Taste* magazine, and have been able to, at points, witness how stories are drawn out of people, attics and furniture, or conjured with a boldness that I continually find inspiring. A dreamlike visit we made to deepest Wales a couple of summers ago sticks in my mind: we were shooting Clough Williams-Ellis's Plas Brondanw garden, as well as some of my knitwear designs amongst the follies and sham ruins. Ruth had already managed (whilst down the pub – where else?) to convince an excellent local potter to model for me, but we were after one more obliging soul. Whilst I, looking at the ground and loitering outside a bookshop with a disposable camera in my raincoat pocket, she, quite seriously, suggested we stop farmers on their tractors in the road.

Details I know others would overlook are pounced upon, for Ruth's magpie eye is persisting and brilliantly hungry for the unusual. A photograph of stacks of boxes in a corridor, say, or a telescopic feather duster propped against a wardrobe, would not make it into most magazines. Obvious choices for her own magazine covers or leading stories are set aside, not for the sake of it, but because there are other, better choices that help tell a story, a story that is deep in detail and rich in atmosphere, and utterly anti-generic.

Stories, of course, are the thing. Stories are what her website, magazine and now this book are all about. These stories of people, home and place woven together by Ruth create, in my mind, a kind of Welsh tapestry blanket of 'Britishness', from the iconic to the esoteric. A bottle of HP Sauce is given as much attention as an ancient Devon tar barrel rolling festival, Ravilious mug or pair of grand and camp swagged curtains. Backed up with a remarkable knowledge of architectural, social and art history, along with a deep understanding of English houses and their owners after years spent working as a curator for English Heritage and story hunter for Rupert Thomas at *The World of Interiors*, Ruth's *Bible* is the result of a very personal investigative journey (albeit one we can all take part in) into what 'Britishness' actually stands for, what our houses, along with our choices of pottery, pictures, food and flowers say about us as individuals, and as a whole.

Luke Edward Hall

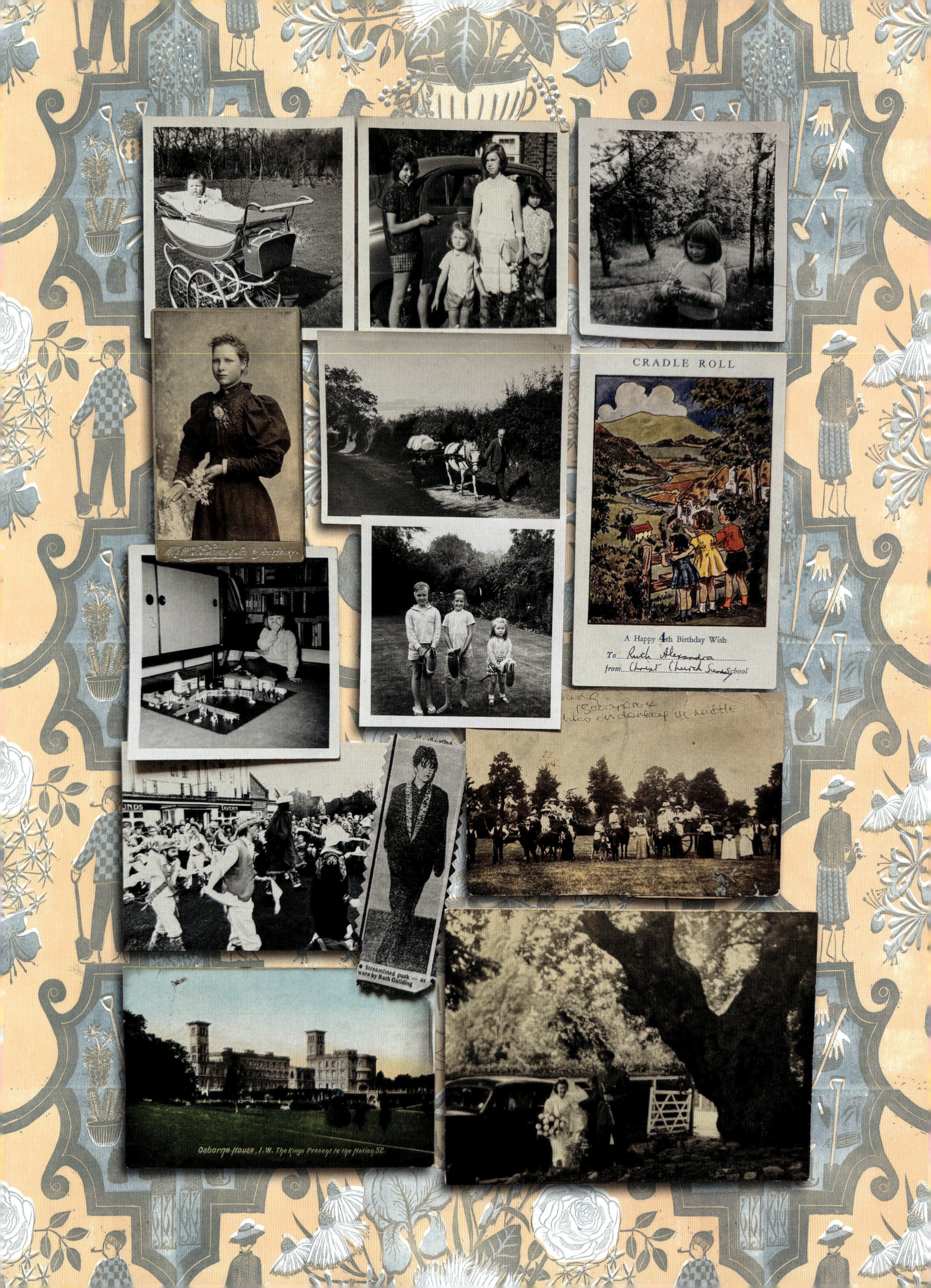
CRADLE ROLL
A Happy 4th Birthday Wish
To Ruth Alexandra
from Christ Church Sunday School
Streamlined punk
worn by Ruth Goulding
Osborne House, I.W. The Kings Present to the Nation.52.

England Made Me

I grew up in a Surrey village swollen by post-war commuting. We were not a very design-conscious family, our furniture upholstered in Sanderson florals, with drab-green fitted carpets and – during my teenage years – a new avocado bathroom suite. There was a kind of unselfconsciousness and freedom in these unexceptional choices, although I was always impressed when my friends' houses revealed more distinctive alternatives to our own aspirational 'normality'.

I was the youngest of my siblings by eight years, having three older sisters. My arrival wasn't planned – my mother had given away the Silver Cross pram to a neighbour, and now supposed, on the balance of probabilities, that the stork had at last decided to deliver a boy. So I grew up in hand-me-downs, benignly bullied by the older ones or left to my own solitary devices. Before I went to school, my 80-year-old grandmother kept an eye on me. She was the eldest of 13 Victorian children born to tenant farmers in rural Buckinghamshire, she'd laboured to bring her siblings into cleanliness and godliness, and I have the Sunday School certificates she was awarded as an exemplary attendee, inscribed to 'Kate Thorne'. Her cooking was very plain; her bath and bedtime routines strict but loving.

No one remembered to teach me to swim, but my father made me a hefty longbow that sent sharpened hazel stakes thrumming into the lawn. We were a bible-reading, church-going family with prayers before bedtime – and, just for me, a top-up Scripture Crusader Class on Sunday afternoons, while the others luxuriated in the BBC's Film for the Family on our new black and white TV, much to my resentment. My education was production-line, at the same schools my sisters had attended. I went first to the dim faux-Scottish primary in our village in inherited uniform – kilt, Fair Isle jumper and battered leather sporran stuffed with hanky and biscuit crumbs – and then to a more prestigious school near Hampton Court, my seven-year-old body fastened into a nine-piece winter uniform (only my Clarks shoes were new). My sisters and I did all share an atavistic craze for the farming life, stemming from our fantasies of my grandmother's childhood on an Aylesbury duck farm and my father's far-off cousins who were in Gloucestershire and in sheep. My mother thought her farming cousins uncouth, but we believed we would have been much happier growing up in rustic naiveté, like the characters of Dodie Smith's novel, *I Capture the Castle* (1948). As the youngest, I had custody of all our three-legged lead farm animals, the new plastic ones for which I saved my pocket money and *The Archers* theme tune lulling me to sleep every night. The ghost of an agricultural past hung on in the village, too: a few sheep and hayfields behind the railway station; Boxing Day Morris dancing; a blacksmith who repaired Shire and Punch lawnmowers and shoed the gymkhana brigade; and the livestock tent at the annual flower show. Acting out our rural fantasies but with no ponies of our own, we cantered around the garden on broomstick 'hobby horses,' whinnying, and whipping our behinds.

Moving On

At 15 years old, punk music and the NME took me out of myself. Wearing an old grandad shirt stencilled with the word 'nihilism' in mixed upper and lower case, my earlobe self-pierced with a safety pin, I pogoed at the church youth group disco. By subterfuge I managed a single gig, secretly changing out of school uniform en route for The Stranglers at Chalk Farm Roundhouse, but slipped sprinting for the last train home and woke up in hospital, concussed. My poor parents marked my card and we lost all faith in one another.

University became my escape route. There was more music and more dressing up, and then, after a couple of fallow years living hand to mouth in Camden Town, I got my first proper job, as regional curator of an out-of-the-way country house for the brand-new government quango English Heritage. (I'd much rather have worked for the National Trust but had come up against an institution still embalmed in a patronage system run by and for tweedy men.) Curators look after the insides of older, richer, dead people's houses; it's a miscellaneous role comprising housekeeper, historian, decorator and jack-of-all-trades, with a great deal of time to look on, consider, appraise and evaluate. I didn't find the cluttered sepia rooms I walked through and worked in aesthetically pleasing, but I did understand exactly how and why they had been made. Reading the sociologist Pierre Bourdieu at university, I had learned to think of the concept of 'good' and 'bad' taste as among the most brilliantly diverting 'constructions' of our long civilisation – eclipsing the History of Art – a whole theatre of compelling, engrossing anthropological study in which we are all knowing or unknowing players. The house I worked in then was of the high Victorian period – and was still frequently described as 'hideous'.

Then the uncommonly astute author Rachel Cusk tore away another veil for me in her essay 'Making Home', describing our houses as the loci of tension and considered design, simultaneously looked at and lived in. She examines our psychological compulsion to make living spaces that reflect us back to ourselves and others – mirages of confected perfection or careless authenticity – and the kudos, pleasure or insecurities stemming from these acts of making as the texts on which we inscribe our dreams and personal mythologies. Reading this, I recognised the subconscious bat squeaks of envy, anxiety or pride that I've been half-listening to for much of my grown-up life. Like Cusk, I am fascinated by the stage sets in which we enact 'home' (so-called 'real homes', not those made by professional decorators) and like her, I think this is a subject worthy of examination and appreciation. And we share a middle-class vantage point that has enabled so many anthropologists, critics, decorators and tastemakers – Peter York, Syrie Maugham, David Hicks, Cecil Beaton, Cusk et al – to look simultaneously upwards and downwards, and draw up critiques that have petrified into touchstones for measuring those chimeras 'distinction' and 'taste'.

Story Hunting

After three years, the diurnal routines of my job curating dead people's houses had begun to pall. Self-employed, *faute de mieux* and now with a master's degree and a doctorate, I was eventually taken on by the non-conformist new editor of *The World of Interiors*, Rupert Thomas, to become a story hunter and writer for the magazine, and set to finding the kind of marvellous tales that the French call *petite histoires*. This turned out to be something I loved doing, permitting a sort of licensed nosiness and a chance to seek out and spend time with an endless variety of people and places I'd otherwise never have known.

At the end of one snowy morning's visit to Frogmore House in Windsor Great Park I was offered a comfort visit to the royal lavatory, then abruptly turned out by the housekeeper as H.M. Queen Elizabeth II announced herself at the French windows on the same errand. Up inside the domes of Brighton's Royal Pavilion I found graffiti scratched by homesick Sikh soldiers hospitalised there during the First World War, and I cooked a scrap lunch for the owners of an astonishingly unrestored medieval priory, scrubbing clean their medieval kitchen sink by way of thanks for my incursion there. I was lent keys to the tiny running-away bolthole of a discreetly Sapphic painter couple high on a Devon cliff and opened damp cupboards and drawers on the antemortem melancholy of their mingled forsaken belongings. My perfectionist editor was a generous employer, but from time to time the stories that I was most invested in – of older silted-up domiciles and long lives well-lived in them – were judged 'not quite right' for publication by Condé Nast. And so, after a little sulking, and a little later on, the idea of the Bible of British Taste floated into my mind: a *salon des refusés* and safe house where I could take the fables, places and people I found that didn't quite fit the template of the magazine world and write about and photograph them 'as found' and just as I pleased. Inevitably it's a limited, self-referencing world, not one that reflects the diversity of contemporary Britain: more backwards facing and conceivably, a little delusional. It follows the trajectory of a narrow childhood in an insular 1960s and 70s Britain, and the niche roles in 'heritage', conservation and journalism that formed my professional life after this. 'The War' cast a long shadow over us, too, for my parents had married in haste and in khaki, their embrace of religious austerity the glue that kept them going afterwards.

Every generation has a different understanding of the word 'British'. Mine – entangled in the associations absorbed from history textbooks and the words of hymns we sang at school assemblies – is out of kilter now, dropping out of sync with today's societal creeds. So I think that the Bible of British Taste is not pretending to be anything more profound than a quest to understand patterns and messages in the lives of others who have lived well or those that strike a chord with me; for after all, what is the point of a house except as a place for settled pleasures and shared generosity, as the vessel holding memories and souvenirs – and for living in? For those who enjoy it, there may be an element of Proustian escapism involved, but these are the stories that have been most pleasing to me or nearest to my heart, and the ones that I have been hunting for, and setting down, ever since.

Part I

Great British Tastemakers

When I was considering how to write about other people's houses, I always thought that the second, gazetteer part of this book would need a prologue, like the two sides of a coin. I thought that this should be something more generalist and more analytical that interrogated a few of the strands in the history of taste that kept recurring in my rudimentary taxonomy of styles. What follows is a kind of bibliography, a look at just three such elements in the last hundred years or so of which I thought I could make sense. Each of them seems to me to exhibit a staying power that makes them endlessly fascinating to each new generation of style hunters, a strong intrinsic aesthetic value and character, and long roots in the recent historical past.

So I singled out: the great pre-Raphaelite William Morris, begetter of the Arts and Crafts movement; the insouciantly individualist and inwardly self-contained artist-members of the Bloomsbury Group; and another quite different phenomenon that had been gradually coming into focus for some time. The latter was how the pioneering architectural Fogeys and squatters of 1970s Spitalfields accidentally reinvented traditional Georgian-era joinery – and its subsequent perfection in the shabby-luxurious New Georgian dream kitchens *de nos jours* by brilliant British brand Plain English. There were plenty of other names and topics that I toyed with and wanted to write about but couldn't quite see so clearly: David Hicks and Terence Conran, Laura Ashley and Cecil Beaton, but I didn't feel best qualified or wasn't sure I had enough of a clear trajectory to do so. The kitchen phenomenon had been blowing about in my head for two or three years as we moved by stops and fitful starts into a third-rate Georgian terraced house where the rooms that would have housed its basement kitchen were a dismal horror film-set, thoroughly dismantled and destroyed. I wanted to make a kitchen we would all spend hours sitting and eating in that was both beautiful and unlike other people's, and perfectly functional and seemed to have existed since the house had been built. Which was patently a falsehood and an impossibility and a nonsense, yet the fantasy stuck. Real Georgians employed domestics and sent their washing out and didn't need white goods: large uncompromising fridges and washing machines.

The pioneer Georgians of 1970s Spitalfields adopted the tenets of 'simple lifers' and frequently did without one or all of these modernities; New Georgians had them all, but skilfully hidden, behind cupboarding, panelling and clever partitions of glass and glazing bars redolent of the pantries and passages of Downton Abbey or a National Trust country house. I simultaneously wanted both or neither and doubted every painfully reached decision and design compromise. In the end the house and the builders fought and won this battle despite and without me, and I write this now sitting at the kitchen table in a room evoking Spencer Gore's 1913 painting *The Gas Cooker* that looks and is authentically old and drably, uncompromisingly plain.

At Home with Mr Morris

Have nothing in your houses that you do not know to be useful, or believe to be beautiful.
Enter, and be happy.

William Morris

I guess he sort of inspired me. He wants people to have the best. ['I do not want art for a few . . . in no private dwelling will there be any signs of waste, pomp, or insolence, and every man will have his share of the best.' – William Morris]

Artist Corbin Shaw

Very Diana Rigg, very Sanderson.

I asked a few friends, 'Why is William Morris still so popular – and ubiquitous?' Few could produce a convincing answer. Most agreed that his patterns and wallcoverings were synonymous with comfort, cosiness, a tranquillity supplied by natural palettes, willow boughs and organic, flowery foliage. Ben Pentreath and I compared notes on our period favourites; his mother had opted to cover their sofa in Morris's classic Willow Boughs, mine chose Golden Lily in the acid-trip blush-orange colourway offered by Sanderson in the 1970s (see right). Twenty years later, in keeping with the zeitgeist, my mother replaced our lumpy horsehair-stuffed Chesterfield with a sleek, new, fire-retardant model from John Lewis, covered in . . . Willow Boughs!

Willow was a pattern that Morris had made from the trees dropping into the river at Kelmscott Manor in Oxfordshire, his summer retreat. His daughter May Morris remembered him pointing out details of the leaf forms and, 'Soon afterwards, this paper was done, a keenly observed rendering of our willows that has embowered many a London living-room.' Ben included several different-coloured versions of this 'Ur-pattern' in his Queen Square collection for Sanderson in 2019–20, returning to some older colourways created by the Sanderson Design Studio and bringing older patterns back into production. We took his second, more vivid Cornubia collection from 2022 to the Prussia Cove estate in west Cornwall for a joyfully clashing Morris & Co. photo shoot that would remain in permanent situ there afterwards, mixing up papers and textiles, tangerine, lemon yellow, primrose, soft pinks, blues and bright apple greens that looked immediately at home – perhaps because they too were the colours and patterns from Ben's mid-70s childhood, a time that sits cheerfully with both full-blown Victorianism and the Arts and Crafts era.

Morris the man

So, who was this William Morris, the beardy socialist from Walthamstow who weltered in a pseudo-medieval dream, the romantic poet with a strongly moral bent, set on improving the lifestyles of the Victorian lower classes? A fantasist, certainly, and an idealist of the very best kind, husband to a swan-necked stableman's daughter, concoctor of self-crafted enchanted worlds at the Red House in Hammersmith, and at Kelmscott Manor, where he exchanged reality for magical escapism. He was the lucky child of city merchants made rich by Devon copper mines, radicalised at Oxford University by fellow undergraduates with Christian Socialist leanings. There, he and Edward Burne-Jones decided to become clergymen and found a religious order or brotherhood to work for the poor in city slums. Their piety was fuelled by close readings of Thomas Malory and other chivalric and virtuous texts. But once they met Dante Gabriel Rossetti, a sensual sexuality gradually pervaded all their doings, disguised as Romantic Love.

There has been so much written since then, so many exhibition catalogues and so much Morris 'stuff' to assess: the companies he founded; the Arts and Crafts architects who carried his baton onwards; the furniture and furnishings made in his own workshops and then by Liberty and other followers – and his patterns (see opposite), still in production and out of copyright, bowdlerised in every weird colourway and scale. So I went back to Kelmscott Manor, the old house Morris found and rented as a summer family retreat, his 'heaven on earth' settled low in Oxfordshire water meadows far from the nearest station or bus stop.

Dark Daisy
11 × 1old Block
001999
Light Daisy
11 × 1old Block
00 1999
Daisy
11 × 1old Block
001999

A Visit to Kelmscott

Morris had loved Kelmscott Manor for its old stone walls that seemed to have 'grown up out of the soil' and 'quaint garrets amongst great timbers of the roof where of old times the tillers and herdsmen slept'. It is still here because his daughter May bequeathed it to the University of Oxford, who passed it into the guardianship of the Society of Antiquaries. May was determined her beloved home should remain forever unchanged. She left strict terms and delimitations on its repair or modernisation, but in the 1960s the university overturned her will in order to pass Kelmscott on.

Long versed in the methods of excavation and conservation, the Antiquaries are staunch disciples of the Society for the Preservation of Ancient Buildings, founded by Morris with good cause in 1877 but now rather zealous in the execution of its brief. Kelmscott is 400 years old, and in common with such ancient places is subject to damp, rot and insect infestation. Six or seven years ago millions of pounds were raised in charitable grants for a major conservation project. The aim is to show us the house brought back to life more authentically, to produce 'a feeling of a house that's lived in rather than a cold, museum-like shrine'. Yet to finance the enterprise, there is a new education centre, larger café, bigger shop, more signage and much, much more bossiness. A stroppy, over-informed visitor like me is parked, queued, scanned, read the rules, held back at the door and enters crepuscular interiors shrouded by blackout blinds and protective netting, Perspex covers and one-way signs (see opposite). Stroppily I go on through all the rooms and back outside, to the outdoor café tables and shop merchandise. Bonsai Strawberry Leaf-patterned oven gloves, fridge magnets, a 'News from Nowhere' tea towel and a crafty heart-shaped lavender bag – the sole nod to the handicrafts Morris furiously championed against all the industrial products that he detested.

But the oven gloves may have their point, for here at Kelmscott, according to his friend Bruce Glasier, Morris claimed to be able to cook, 'bake bread and brew ale with any farmer's wife in Oxfordshire' – highly abnormal accomplishments for a man of his class. And for modern Morris-lovers this is part of the great attraction – this lifestyle, this espousal of 'simplicity of life'. At Kelmscott, as Morris describes in *News from Nowhere*, 'Everywhere there was but little furniture, and that only the most necessary, and of the simplest forms.' The sumptuous things – such as old tapestries, his wife Jane's luxurious four-poster bed and her painted jewel casket – were set off by medieval-style austerity, whitewash and utility. Maud Sambourne (daughter of the Punch cartoonist Linley Sambourne) complained to her mother in 1896, that, 'The house is lovely for its oldness but oh! so so artistic . . . We sat in a row in the plain, painfully plain dining room' (the manor's old entrance hall). The chairs now in the room are the rush-seated, ebonised, quasi-peasant 'Sussex' chairs sold in huge quantities by Morris, Marshall, Faulkner & Co. from 1866, copied with modifications from an old village chair picked up in Sussex and a favourite with their middle-class customers.

Designs for a new Uptopia

In his 1880 lecture on 'Making the Best of It', Morris was firmly prescribing simplicity: 'We must clear our houses of troublesome superfluities that are forever in our way.' The secret was a kind of utilitarianism, to have a few things of 'honesty' and high quality, well made, with beautiful surface decoration or finish. In another of that year's lectures Morris advised that, 'Simplicity of life, even the barest, is not a misery but the very foundation of refinement.' No matter if walls were hung with costly tapestry, whitewashed or paper-patterned, 'if it were done for beauty's sake and not for show'. But also, 'All rooms ought to look as if they were lived in.' Then he produced his golden rule, the one that's now – by paradox – reproduced on every fridge magnet in Kelmscott's gift shop: 'Have nothing in your houses that you do not know to be useful, or believe to be beautiful.'

Beauty was key for Morris, something he could achieve with comparative ease by extraordinary artistic skill and considerable purchasing power. At his riverside house in Hammersmith, the sumptuous blue drawing room on the first floor – with his woven woollen Bird fabric curtaining its walls from picture rail to floor and Oriental carpets (see top right)– was a show house for his decorating firm: important clients entered and were utterly seduced. But the kind of performative 'simplicity' which he strongly advocated was much more achievable in a holiday house like Kelmscott, whose inmates were licensed and leisured to 'play' at life there. The point Morris laboured was to be 'anti' all things Victorian: superfluity, pretentiousness, conspicuous consumption.

Morris's patterns bring the outside inside, 'the force that through the green fuse drives the flower' pulsing with organic life. His 1880s textile designs were named for local tributaries of the River Thames, such as the Kennet (see previous page). His ever-popular Daisy design (see page 15) comes from flower motifs adapted by Morris from those painted in miniature in a fifteenth-century manuscript, *Froissart's Chronicles*, that Jane and family stitched into bedroom wall hangings on a length of indigo-dyed serge.

Customers, Followers and Disciples

Morris saw himself as a conduit, bringing back these centuries-old traditions in art and design disrupted by the Industrial Revolution, but as his small-scale interior design company Morris, Marshall, Faulkner & Co. changed and expanded, he grew more divided, simultaneously reformist missionary, businessman and manufacturer. The middle-class Kensington house of artist-cartoonist-designer Linley Sambourne bears witness to this mass-market appeal, for the Sambournes spent freely to give it the 1880s all-over Aesthetic Movement look, papering their morning room with Morris's Fruit or Pomegranate paper on walls and ceiling in two contrasting colourways. The other side of the coin, the skilled craftsman reproducing decorative techniques from the Middle Ages, survives miraculously in the modest Cambridge home of David Parr, artist-painter working for the specialist firm F.R. Leach & Sons. His company executed decorative paintwork on commission for Morris & Co. in larger houses and churches, with craftsman-cypher Parr returning home to carefully hand-paint and adapt Morris's designs all over the walls of his own small rooms.

Morris means different and important things to the contemporary designers who rate him highly. I asked Marthe Armitage, who began drawing and hand printing wallpaper 50 years ago (see bottom right), what she thought of him. She wrote in reply:

As you say, I am not really a disciple, but I owe him a lot, so here goes: As a pattern maker, my first inspiration was William Morris and he, I think, was set off by those wonderful textiles from India. His perfectly symmetrical patterns are endlessly satisfying and made me feel he had had the last word. Except – were not his designs a bit over controlled? Could not the plants he used be set free to trail over the wall and yet be coaxed into a repeat? I put together a primitive printing method, found an angelica plant growing outside, and that was the start. I thought I didn't love W.M. but I do.

Like me, artist and interior designer Laurence Llewelyn-Bowen had a Morris-y childhood. Over the phone he told me:

I remember the moment my mother introduced William Morris into our minimalist lives in the 60s, a three-piece suite arrived – the kinkiest thing I'd seen in my life – undulating kinky photosynthesis going on. Socialism was important to her sense of social responsibility – and one of the big things about Morris is that he comes with a soft Fabianism that people love. So he became an icon and rallying point for the middle classes. He did something in the history of patternmaking that no one else did, took his inspiration from fourteenth- and fifteenth-century Italian damasks – the sinuous nature of a line that crosses from left to right, that feels like a beanstalk, muscular, growing to the light. And Morris is so damn practical, not foreign or poncey at all.

Morris was briefly out of vogue in the 90s but he never has a revival – because he is a consistent survivor. His style is muscular – something that Laura Ashley never understood – he understood that nature is big and bosomy; hedgerows are full of things that prick you as well as flowers; life cycles end in entropy and morbidity as decadent, stinky compost. The designers House of Hackney borrow heavily from Morris, theirs is a kitsch, disco version of Morris. My reinterpretation is more acid house, a gaudy garden of earthly delights, fertile nature and roses round the door, a soft-porn Arthurian idyll.

As Lawrence and I – children of the 1960s and 70s – well know, twentieth-century Morris became the first choice for decor in middle-class homes all over England. When Morris & Co. finally closed in 1940, its designs continued to be sold under licence (and the Morris & Co. brand) by Sanderson & Sons and by Liberty of London. Post-Second World War, chilly Modernism and Brave New World tendencies sent many rushing back into nostalgia. In the words of style commentator Stephen Bayley (who despises Morris), 'Morris had looked all the way back to the thirteenth century, now Little England looked back to Morris, and the German émigré scholar Nikolaus Pevsner encouraged them to think of him as a visionary pioneer of modern design and workable social theories.'

But clever, cool, smart style-innovators saw the fun and fashion in Victorian Revivalism, and by 1957 socialite Anne Parsons, Countess of Rosse, was giving a party to found the Victorian Society in Linley Sambourne House with Victorian fancier John Betjeman in attendance; later, Pevsner and the decorator John Fowler joined up too. A few miles away, actor Peter Cook's first wife, Wendy, was papering their Georgian terraced house in Hampstead in all-over Morris. Sanderson's mid-70s advertising campaign featured slinky actress Diana Rigg's Golden Lily-upholstered modernist sofa and smoked-glass coffee table: 'Very Diana Rigg, very Sanderson' (see page 14). Chrysanthemum (see page 20), Golden Lily, Willow and Blackthorn were the patterns that everyone was choosing then, as the quantities of second-hand 'sill length' 60s- and 70s-period curtains now for sale on eBay confirm.

Curiously, two of these quintessentially Morris-y patterns were not designed by Morris at all, for medievalising Golden Lily (1899) and Blackthorn (1892, originally produced as a fabric) were both recently confirmed as the work of John Henry Dearle, ex weaver turned inspired Head Designer at Morris & Co. whose synthetic, sinuous pattern-making chimed exactly with Pop Arty 60s and 70s taste. Wallpaper remains the most accessible way to furnish with Morris's designs, and the helpful advice he supplied in numerous public lectures is still relevant:

> *If there is a reason for keeping the walls quiet choose a pattern that works well all over without pronounced lines, such as the Diapers, Mallows, Venetians, Poppy, Scroll, Jasmine etc . . . If you venture on a more decided patterning you ought always to go for positive patterns when they may be had, choose the Daisy, Trellis [see page 18], Vine, Chrysanthemum, Lily, Honeysuckle, Larkspur, Rose, Acanthus or such. In deciding between those whose direction or set is horizontal, and those which have more obviously vertical or oblique lines, you must be guided entirely by the look of the room.*

Successes and Failures

As social reformer, Morris was a Utopian failure. In his eco-socialist paradise, a dignified classless society would live anti-capitalist and anti-commercial lives in harmony with one another and with nature, and 'there will be no compulsion on us to go on producing things we do not want'. This has not come to pass. The affluent classes are still fluent in Morris. His exhortations to 'treat the natural beauty of the earth as a holy thing', 'to bring together the makers and the buyers of goods as closely as possible', are the mantras of those who shop for artisan bread and organic milk at farmers' markets and pieces of beautifully handmade clothing or studio pottery. But as Corbin Shaw has pointed out, we are presently living in a 'Little Dark Age', an antithesis to Morris's world vision, full of cheap, crap goods manufactured from the earth's dwindling resources by sweated labour and sent round the world in shipping containers – smashed-up patio heaters and Ikea furniture thrown out on the pavements on bin day.

Then as now, William Morris remains one of the most engaging operators in the decorating marketplace. The briar roses, pomegranates, birds and prickly thorns of his two-dimensional designs tangle in our thoughts with the sickly-sweet romanticism of his damsels and knights and arras-hung rooms. The things he craved, hoarded and collected are grander, older examples of things we may aspire to live among – rustic Sussex chairs, William De Morgan tiles and older, craftsman-made things from Islamic cultures that, Morris said, contribute their romance by 'making the past part of the present'. Above all, in a Morris-y room, there's harmony, no dissonance.

At Kelmscott, in the ground-floor room once known as the Green Room and hung with Morris's faded green Kennet chintz, there's a good, dark Brunswick Green paint, a blended Prussian blue and chrome yellow colour that Morris found 'restful to the eyes', recreated for Kelmscott by historical paint consultant Patrick Baty. The green colour continues through the rooms of the ground floor and stops at the first floor, with its larger, lighter rooms and windows to the sky. As I write this, unctuous deep-green rooms have been trending on Instagram for several years now with goose shit and grass and sea-weedy spectrums predominating, the early adopters seeding algorithms that have been picked up by almost every interior decorator and amateur worth their salt. A souped-up pea-green 'Autumn' colourway from Ben Pentreath's recent Queens Square collection for Morris & Co. pays homage to the original deep base colour of the Blackthorn wallpaper that J.H. Dearle designed for Morris & Co. in 1892. Alan Bennett and Virginia Woolf both chose to live in rooms suffused with green. Trying for a DIY grassier green, I had accidentally mixed and made a full tin of faux-Brunswick Green last year and set it crossly aside as suitable only for repainting a Chieftain tank, but now I see things differently.

Back to Morris and his organic roots. I am doing him homage, trying samples from Morris & Co. here and there about the house. I like his Brer Rabbit pattern (see opposite) and of course I like the 70s revival colours bringing back my past into present – and Morris's ideal-fantasy past – the safer, known place where we can enter and 'be happy'.

Bloomsbury: Character is Everything

The wealthy flat owner, distrusting his own taste, engages the 'experts' of a furniture shop to design, deliver and dispose about the rooms the elements which, as the expression of his own individuality, would have made it a home.

Duncan Grant

There is *echt* Bloomsbury, and there is Bloomsbury. The inner circle belong to Sussex, the households of Virginia Woolf and her painter sister Vanessa Bell, and, perhaps, to the Wiltshire homestead where painter Dora Carrington kept house for writer and critic Lytton Strachey. Then there are the outer concentric rings, the various London houses they rented periodically around Fitzrovia, those of Bloomsbury gurus, friends, lovers and acolytes such as painter and critic Roger Fry and the Stracheys. And posh Bloomsbury, with houses that were older and more distinguished – Lady Ottoline Morrell at Garsington Manor, Bryan Guinness at Biddesden, the MacCarthys at Wiveton. Poshest of all was Eddy Sackville-West, heir to the whole of the ancient Knole estate in Kent. Shabby-posh Bloomsbury was a kind of watered-down Arts and

Crafts aesthetic where Fabians and intellectuals cohabited with Morris patterns, mothy tapestries and thick white dinner services designed by Roger Fry. They existed beyond the diaspora, a more dilute concentration of the ethos.

By a miracle, several Bloomsbury domains, most notably Charleston Farmhouse (see opposite) and Monk's House (see above), survive more or less intact. Informally written diary entries and letters of the group's inner coterie give us a much more intimate sense of how their houses were put together and the 'group think' governing why certain interior-related decisions were made.

Virginia Woolf at home, Monk's House in Sussex

Monk's House was Virginia Woolf's shockingly original and carefully schemed-out characterful creation. Importantly, it was simple and unpretentious, writing in her diary, she called it – 'an unpretending house, long and low'. Over about 20 years, beginning in 1919, Woolf ordered 16 alterations to this poky little eighteenth-century cottage until it was a much larger, lighter space with an informal semi-open-plan ground floor.

Its furnishings were accomplished *en famille*: three years after the Woolfs bought the house at auction, Vanessa Bell and painter and designer Duncan Grant set up a house decorating business from Grant's Fitzrovia studio. With her earnings from the success of her book *Orlando* in 1929 and Vita Sackville-West's Hogarth Press novels, Virginia bought their ceramics and textiles and commissioned bespoke furniture for her reception rooms at Monk's House – a couple of tables, one painted, one set with Grant's tiles, the set of lilac-painted and caned chairs picked out in contrasting colours by her sister that sit with it, and furniture painted yellow, pink and terracotta left over from an unsuccessful selling exhibition at the Lefevre Gallery. A set of chair seats were stitched with their daughter Angelica's designs of Leda and the Swan, everything set off against walls painted a saturated cobalt shade of Scheele's green and hung with dozens of Bloomsbury paintings.

Woolf's most ambitious improvement was to add on the all-important ground-floor workroom and 'room of one's own' that doubled as her bedroom (see below), with a winter sitting room above it. It is lined with bookcases and a calmer pale green distemper that is almost white. Vanessa painted its charmingly poetic fireplace tiles with a vignette of a sailing ship and lighthouse in remembrance of their childhood holidays and Virginia's eponymous novel, and signed it, 'VW from VB 1930'.

The 1930s were the apogee of her scheme's perfection, her Petit Trianon era, for Monk's House was not created for quotidian living. As with Charleston, the house was a 'second home' for entertaining and retreat at weekends, Christmas, Easter and the summer months each year that then became their permanent residence in wartime. When, in 1940, the house that they had rented in Tavistock Square was bombed, London furniture and possessions arrived to crowd the sparse perfection of the rooms in Sussex.

Few of us would care to admit to 'house shame', the fear of being judged by the house in which we live, or other kinds of painful self-consciousness. Woolf felt herself vulnerable to all of them. As someone whose writing practice was posited on observing – 'seeing people among their things' – and judging others, she was acutely tuned to the power that surroundings and objects could exert. Woolf wrote in her diary of feeling compelled to leave her writing room every half hour to look at a new chest of drawers she had just bought. She often described clothes, furniture and houses, sometimes doubting her own choices and tastes, for her intellectual self-belief could be counter-weighted by debilitating insecurities like the movement of a clock pendulum. But the rooms she had made at Monk's House brought her a particular

satisfaction. Returning home from Vita's Long Barn with its butler, antiques and much higher standards of comfort, Woolf wrote in her diary, 'I like this room better, perhaps more effort and life in it, in my mind, unless this is the prejudice one has naturally in favour of the display of one's own character.' And her competitive satisfaction in her own unique way of decorating – trumping her sister Vanessa even? – must have been confirmed when her brother-in-law Clive Bell told her that she had 'created an atmosphere different from, perhaps better than, any I know.'

Manufacturing Bloomsbury and the Omega Workshop

A century on, Bloomsbury's interior style is an established market and fertile territory for anyone trying to anatomise mores and fashions in household decoration. But where did their very particular way of 'making home' come from? Partly, from a reaction, for Bloomsbury had been in revolt against the pervasive Victorianism that had clung to their houses and family customs and, in this, Roger Fry had a significant role as their guru and tastemaker.

Brought up in a strict Quaker household, Fry's austere preference was for uncarpeted rooms with bare polished-wood floors decorated in pale greys and dull greens – an Arts and Crafts aesthetic but without what he dubbed its moral earnestness – because, he said, 'We have suffered too long from the stupidly serious.' Fry had set up the Omega Workshops to infuse the dullness and formality of Edwardian interior decoration with a modernist, painterly approach, 'to keep the spontaneous freshness of primitive or peasant work while satisfying the needs and expressing the feelings of modern cultivated man'.

Spontaneity was key and far more important than high aptitude or skill. Fry's artists and art students worked on furniture, ceramics and book illustrations as well as painting and sculpture, painting Fauvist, Cubist-style surface pattern onto furniture, lamps, trays, pottery, tiles and boxes, signing their work only with the Greek letter 'O'. Omega's early colour schemes and combinations were violent, described scathingly by a friend of C.R. Ashbee as 'pink, acid mauve, lemon and a sort of cocoa colour'. Keeping things primitive and 'peasanty', Omega artists must not spoil the expressive qualities of their work by sandpapering it down to a high, shop finish.

Vanessa Bell and Duncan Grant at home, Charleston Farmhouse, Sussex

At home at Charleston, Bell and Grant continued to embellish Fry's pared-back domestic style with the lavishly applied surface decoration that characterised Omega's furniture and ceramics (see pages 26–27). Some of their furniture was brought down from London, and cheap pieces that could be all-over painted were picked up at the auction house in Lewes. Unconventionality was the norm: Bell co-habited with Grant, while her husband Clive Bell came and went along with other inmates and lovers.

In wartime isolation, Bell and Grant became more and more preoccupied with milieu. Paint was transformational and everything is smothered in it. Woolf commented, perhaps rather critically, 'every inch of the house is a different colour'. In common with Monk's House, there is an aesthetic of floorboards and rugs, art, textiles and ceramics. Bell told Fry that she was trying to carry out the idea that she had always had of 'bedrooms with the minimum of furniture'. But souvenirs of intelligent foreign travel were incorporated into Bloomsbury-made interiors, too. Woolf had spent some of her surplus earnings on furniture and ceramics that she bought on French holidays; novelist Elizabeth Bowen remembered her at Rodmell sitting on the floor mending a torn Spanish curtain. Bell and Grant looked to Italian motifs; when first domiciled at Charleston, both were busy painting copies of Italian primitives. There's a pretty eighteenth-century Venetian console table in Charleston's dining room, artisan pottery from Spain and France, and large-thighed classical nudes embellish the sitting-room overmantel and Painting Studio chimneypiece (see page 22).

Yet Charleston was an ever-changing canvas, for these were living spaces in a constant state of flux, adapted to the dynamic

needs of family and communal life, the settled and the temporary, and to the business of making art. There were decorative schemes dating from the onset that were freshened or repainted later, and more coherent redecorating, moving out of Fauvist tendencies into their own signature style in the 1920s after their lease on the house was extended and the household settled in. Charleston's painting studio added in 1925 is miraculously preserved with its easel, brush pots and inspirational bric-a-brac-laden mantlepiece (see pages 22 and 26). Bloomsbury aficionado Isabelle Anscombe's book *Omega and After* (1981) shows this room and the others prior to Charleston's takeover and clean-up, when Quentin Bell still had nominal charge; a cluttered, tattered and *deshabille* interior with piles of papers and crockery covering its painted tabletops. When the household retrenched there permanently in 1939, Duncan Grant and Quentin Bell had applied stencilled decoration to the dining-room walls; Vanessa painted the dining-room tabletop and made the extraordinarily beautiful curtains out of mismatched patterned chintzes (see opposite). In the 1940s she stencilled a serene grey and white paisley pattern onto the drawing-room walls – repetitive, therapeutic work accomplished at a time of grief for the deaths of her sister and eldest son.

Immured at Charleston and preoccupied with the joint project of its all-over decoration, Vanessa and Duncan had soon dropped out of the Omega experiment. Without them and in wartime, Omega Workshop's attempt at selling to a wider public had foundered after just six years of trading. Omega had been over-reliant on the support of Bloomsbury's friends and London's literary and artistic coterie, the things it sold were expensive, *outré* and seemed ridiculous to outsiders. Twenty-six years later, in his novel *Brideshead Revisited*, Evelyn Waugh sketched the Damascene moment when Charles Rider realises the painted Omega screen in his college rooms shows a horrible lack of taste. Grander Bloomsbury friends and patrons had shopped at Omega, but when it came to more site-specific artworks or schemes they went bespoke to individual artists.

Biddesden House is another Bloomsbury country house. Bryan Guinness bought it soon after his marriage to Diana Mitford, when both were in their early twenties. Dora Carrington was already established with her guru and soulmate Lytton Strachey a few miles away at Ham Spray. Between them they had many more friends in the Bloomsbury coterie – the portrait painter Henry Lamb who was a chum of Duncan Grant's, Grant's sometime lover the sculptor Stephen Tomlin and the aristocratic Russian mosaicist Boris Anrep.

All of these artists created work for Biddesden: a glorious pool house mosaiced by Anrep (see opposite, bottom right); a larger-than-life garden statue of Pomona by Tomlin; and Carrington's trompe l'oeil window scene painted on one of the house's external blocked-up windows in 1931. Inside, the rooms and corridors retain a strong – if subtler – Bloomsbury sensibility, with panelling picked out in blues, pinks and yellows, Bloomsbury hand-painted lampshades, carpets by the textile designer Marion Dorn and shelves of china plates backed with the deep Marie Laurencin pink favoured by Eddy Sackville-West (see opposite).

Wiveton Hall is a Bloomsbury house by proxy, connected by inheritance to Molly MacCarthy (aka Mary, Lady MacCarthy, married to the journalist and writer Desmond MacCarthy). It was she who coined the nickname 'Bloomsberries' in 1910, which was adopted by a cohort of her male Cambridge-educated friends as a private joke. In 1948 her son, Desmond, married Chloe Buxton, daughter of the house, who lived at Wiveton from 1972 until her son, also Desmond, came of age. This house still refers back to Bloomsbury, with yellow, pink and blue paintwork and a library-ballroom full of their books and paintings. Desmond's painter sister Mary MacCarthy keeps the Bloomsbury pilot light burning too, in a nearby flint-faced, low-ceilinged farmhouse that's saturated with colour, painted furniture and pottery.

Twenty-first century Bloomsbury

With Monk's House and Charleston both 'saved' as heritage and sites of pilgrimage for almost half a century now, everyone can see Bloomsbury's way with colour, paint and surface decoration, spontaneity and rough, DIY finishes, for themselves. To recreate something in this spirit is far from easy, though. There are some reproductions for sale, Laura Ashley was licensed to sell a collection of Bloomsbury fabric designs in 1985 to celebrate the saving of Charleston, and there are eight of Bell and Grant's document patterns for sale in the on-site Charleston shop. But Bloomsbury is never 'matchy matchy', and shops are not the places from which household things should be sourced. Makers include Cressida Bell, who has been selling Bloomsbury lampshades for decades and has spawned many imitators; and David Herbert who has become a successful ceramicist by channelling the spirit of Bloomsbury pottery.

Even so, these are only charming pastiches of the authentic originals; unconventional domesticity demands much more. Character, individuality and self-expression are Bloomsbury's watchwords; hand-painted and repainted surfaces are proofs of spontaneity and originality. The things you live among must be old, rustic or crafted amateur-style by you or a lover or an artist in your circle. Professional interior decorators have no place here. Books and pictures should be written and painted, given and bought: every Bloomsbury household is full of them. Writer Alan Bennett began hand-painting and staining his walls with greenish inks and varnishes from the Camden Town artists colour shop in 1968, his rooms already housing quantities of books, paintings and old furniture. The effects are rather evocative of the 'second-generation Omega' Cambridge college rooms of Bloomsbury-ite Dadie Rylands, where 'absolutely Bloomsbury' greys, magentas, bitter yellow, dowdy greens and dusty pinks were mottled, stippled and painted over every surface.

Charleston farmhouse, with its palimpsest of all-over decoration, is still brimming with a posthumous mystique, feted in *Vogue*, honoured as an enclave of queer sexuality by fashion writer Charlie Porter (*Bring No Clothes*, 2023) and inspiring recent collections for Dior and Fendi. The fashion label Toast publishes blog posts about Bloomsbury on its website, *The Guardian* carries the headline 'Get the Charleston look: How to give your home a Bloomsbury makeover'. Bloomsbury style is always bohemian, with strong intellectual pretensions and anti-normative sexuality. We know that when Vita or Eddy Sackville-West, Lytton Strachey, E.M. Forster or other highbrow guests called at Monk's House, the talk was as informal and performatively unconventional as the rooms and their furniture, dwelling on Sapphic love or copulation and sodomy while Virginia smoked a cheroot or embroidered one of her sister's avant garde designs onto a square of canvas.

In the stock market of culture, Bloomsbury still broadcasts this manifesto of personal and sexual freedom of expression, superior liberal and aristocratic values and painterly aesthetics, via the books, artefacts, houses and professional proselytisers left behind. Houses *are* important, character is *everything*. Orotund Leonard Woolf, guardian of the Monk's House shrine for 48 years after Virginia's suicide, supplies the last word:

> *What has the deepest and most permanent effect upon oneself and one's way of living is the house in which one lives. The house determines the day-to-day, hour-to-hour, minute-to-minute quality, colour, atmosphere, pace of one's life; it is the framework of what one does, of what one can do, and of one's relations with people.*

Spitalfields Fogeys, New Georgians and the Invention of Plain English

In my early twenties I lived in a shared house in Camden, part of a pretty little terrace of houses from the 1800s that was notionally run by a housing co-op. The other side of the street housed council tenants. Our side had been squatted, knocked about and condemned, the local council passing up the tricky job of bringing these houses up to modern standards; we paid almost no rent. There wasn't a supply of hot water but in the basements most of the original built-in Georgian-style dressers, kitchen ranges and chipped ceramic butler's sinks remained in situ. After a few months, one enterprising ex-squatter gouged out and sold the best of them to a Camden Lock antiques dealer for just enough to pay off his drug debts. We were used to furnishing our rooms with things gleaned from skips, but when I got a starter job at the Royal Commission for Historic Monuments I became fanatical about period interiors.

Circa 1985 I was in the front row at a Saturday Study Day in the Truman Brewery building in Spitalfields to be lectured by the heroes of the 1970s campaign to save its early Georgian houses from the developer's wrecking balls (see right). A cabal of conservation warriors, including the historian Raphael Samuel and architectural historians Mark Girouard and Dan Cruickshank, were the speakers. I listened, mesmerised by the romance of those pioneer 'settlers' who had reclaimed these buildings from dereliction, dodging the wrecking balls, burning skip wood in their kitchen ranges, salvaging original shutters and panelling from houses that had already been torn down, cooking by candlelight in verminous basements.

Spitalfields was still the authentic slum described by a shocked Charles Dickens in the 1830s, home to half a dozen migrant communities, the market traders' rotten fruit and veg strewn across its pavements, the pubs open all night to serve their early morning thirst, the tramps attracted by the nocturnal bustle. The Huguenot merchants and master weavers who fled here from France at the end of the seventeenth century were subsequently replaced by Jewish tailors and furriers, Irish weavers and then, a descent into poverty and criminality; finally, immigrants from Bangladesh settled here and set up restaurants in the 1970s and 80s. But bohemian gentrification was coming, the artists Gilbert and George conducting their parody of marital domesticity in Fournier Street from the late 1960s ('In our art and in our life, I think we are very interested in that that is discarded or disguised or discredited').

Eventually, the Spitalfields Historic Buildings Trust founded in 1977 by Cruickshank and others began to purchase condemned houses from the developers who threw them back onto the market, sensing that their game might be up. More houses were rescued and sold on with covenants to sympathetic new owners, many of them to the trust's associates and employees. Dan first entered his future home at 15 Elder Street in the mid-70s, finding parts of it long abandoned, the basement knee-deep in debris and rubbish. The evidence for its last period of sustained use was a calendar pinned to a cupboard door and dated 1944. The flamboyant Canadian Dennis Severs bought no. 18 Folgate Street (a house dating from 1724) from the Spitalfields Trust in 1979 and spent the next 20 years conjuring his theatrical chronology of the imaginary Jervis family there, 'a historical three-dimensional novel, written in brick and candlelight' charting the lives of its residents through 170 years, up until the death of Queen Victoria (see opposite). Owner, curator and tour guide combined, Severs was notorious for his abusive treatment of any paying visitors who failed to 'get it'; his house with room sets all intact now operates as a more benign tourist attraction.

Later on, my friendships with Dan Cruickshank, the designer Marianna Kennedy and architectural historian Will Palin took me inside other houses there. The original Spitalfields settlers lived sans heating and utilities, recreating unfitted Victorian slum kitchens of startling beauty from salvage, pioneering the Belfast sink and wooden draining board, oil lamps, open kitchen ranges, flagstones and scrubbed pine. Will's Hanbury Street house had come with a full-sized tree trunk propping up his collapsing staircase. Mariana had made an extraordinarily beautiful home and showroom from what had once been a banana warehouse in Fournier Street, where Rupert Thomas staged a party for *The World of Interiors*. Second-generation settlers were moving in: artist Tracey Emin, decorator-author Jocasta Innes and writer Jeanette Winterson arrived.

From Gentrification to Boom

With this gentrification came a property boom, when shabby and part-restored houses were sold on to the deeper pockets of adventurous young lawyers, bankers and city traders who enjoyed the area's residual edginess and proximity to their work but were less sympathetic to its shabby patina. Meanwhile the diaspora was spreading out to next-door London neighbourhoods. By 1999 *The Guardian* cartoonist Posy Simmonds' central characters in her comic-strip story *Gemma Bovery* (a former magazine illustrator and a furniture restorer) were living frugally among piles of *The World of Interiors* with 'real eighteenth-century dust' between the floorboards – 'Hogarthy, smoke-blackened, cosy-shabby, all sort of clay pipes and piss pots' – in a pregentrified, postcode-adjacent Hackney, which was 'really buzzy and full of artists'.

Even so, 'Spitalfields life' remained a minority interest until 2009, when an enterprising character calling himself 'the Gentle Author' arrived and started to blog about it. His eponymous website was wholly original, telling the stories of the buildings, their history and the characters both alive and dead that had lived here. He gained a global audience, employed writers and researchers, and published a book of the same name (see above) while protecting the mystique of his anonymity. Suddenly all sorts of fascinating information and photographs were there to be harvested at the click of a mouse. As the last working-class pubs, cafés and trade warehouses folded, Spitalfields was being thoroughly commodified, featuring in more and more coffee-table books and magazine articles. The eternal glamour of 'authenticity', deeply patinated wood, worn floorboards, palimpsests of broken paintwork and unique joinery crafted by long-dead craftsmen – set off by a single candlestick on a worn wooden table, an eloquent light sconce, a humble pewter plate, half a rustic loaf and *always* a butler's sink – was offered up as a fashionable interior-decorating stylistic choice.

© Derry Moore

Architectural Fogeys and New Georgians

Meanwhile, all over England, architectural historians and 'New Georgians' had been remaking their homes in the spirit of historical reconstruction, pioneers of gentrification bringing up families in the unloved and unlovely places where boarded up and multi-occupied old housing stock survived and could be had cheap. In the red-light district around London's St Pancras Station, Gavin and Alex Stamp rebuilt the marble fireplaces in their sooty terraced house and burned coal and skip wood in the grates (see above). Stamp wrote gloatingly in Derry Moore's photographic record The Englishman's Room (1980) of how his house had survived any modernisation, with its original doors, staircase and cornices all intact. They had stripped off old wallpaper to reveal bare plaster: 'to get a clever stainer and grainer to achieve this decaying palazzo effect would be very expensive. As it is, it is very economical, as is the treatment of the joinery. The Bloomsbury mottled finish is achieved by the inept use of a blow-lamp.' The movement's manifesto was *The New Georgian Handbook* (1985) written by Stamp's first wife, Alexandra Artley, and John Martin Robinson and published by Harpers & Queen. They had already set out their stall in *The Spectator* on 22 December 1984, in an article entitled 'Kentucky Fried Georgian':

> *To repair their houses properly, Fogeys invented architectural salvage. Miles away when philistines are gutting an old house, Fogeys pick up high-frequency distress signals. Suddenly, they are there, saving the bits if they can't actually stop the destruction . . . When a demolition pickaxe shatters the work of the human hand, Fogeys feel it is a blow against humanity. If an old house is modernised with a new crudely-panelled front door, Fogeys call the style Kentucky Fried Georgian . . .*

Fogey families believe in conservation heroics. They live with no roof, then no floors, then only a few walls, but lots of dry rot, Greek builders drinking Coca-Cola, collapsing ceilings, cold water, layers of filth, cellars full of old tights and tea-leaves, re-wiring by day, re-plumbing by fly-by-night and donating the drawing room as an emergency campaign office. Fogeys learned to rough it in the early Seventies. They trained as conservation commandos in squats and Direct Action against London's rapacious property developers.

Their friends the artists Glyn and Carrie Boyd Harte had found a derelict terraced house in Cloudesley Square in Islington, where historian John Martin Robinson met them for supper arriving at an 'uninhabitable Georgian wreck' where they removed a bit of rusty corrugated iron, climbed in and then ate a picnic together off the floor. Its finished interiors featured a great deal of wood-graining, about which the GBH's were evangelical in an age of universally stripped pine. They appear in *The New Georgian Handbook* as 'Mr. and Mrs. Soanie' among the standard Fogey attributes of bare boards and exquisite marble (working!) fireplace, with a tiny Eric Ravilious Wedgwood mug poised in the middle of their floor.

In Suffolk, Richard and Tricia Hewlings moved their young family into the semi-derelict Big Old House, as it was known locally – a beaten-up farmhouse that had been subdivided into flats for the workers who ran a tractor-tyre retreading factory from its concreted yards. It's built of red brick, and is flat-fronted with a pretty Georgian doorcase and an older wing jettying out into what was once the farmyard at the rear. Richard (formerly an Inspector of Ancient Monuments for Historic England) filled it with old joinery and furniture, the by-products of a lifetime's salvaging and curiosity for old things and buildings.

They had employed Jim Howett, an extraordinary young American craftsman and joiner (who has been living and working in Spitalfields ever since) to make and mend its broken rooms, and it was here that I first encountered the phenomenon of a 'New Georgian' kitchen – something that looked as old as the house, almost, and yet a little too streamlined and considered for that to be plausible. The kitchen straggled across two good-sized rooms; there were two old dressers, a pine table, a linen press, a metal meat safe cupboard and – filling one entire wall – a symphony of joinery, homage to the kitchen sink (see top left). Painted an ochre ox-blood colour, it was hand built, partly by Richard, with display shelves for china and a long plate rack directly above the ceramic butler's sink; cupboards and drawers beneath; and a lead splashback designed by Tricia. In fact, it looked very like an early prototype or template for a company I had first come across in the 1990s and been watching ever since. Around then, in a clapboarded seaside house, some West Country builders had made a very plain, handsome kitchen for us based on my back-of-an-envelope drawings. These drawings were copied with small amendments from a brochure that I keep carefully in a drawer and the name on that brochure is – 'Plain English, Cupboardmakers' (see bottom left).

The Invention of Plain English

But the genius inventors of Plain English Design did not live in Spitalfields. Katie Fontana and Tony Niblock were not provincial but they too were in the provinces, building a traditional Suffolk

longhouse. Katie could not find anything to buy in the way of appropriately plain, vernacular kitchen joinery and so set out to design her own, based upon the patterns of below-stairs rooms in seventeenth- and eighteenth-century buildings and built by a local joiner. Then she found that a new brand calling itself The Shaker Shop had opened in London selling just what she needed but at prices beyond her reach. Yet the stylistic elements of Shaker and its philosophy of simplicity, functionality and craftsmanship mirrored the kinds of beautifully pared-back architectural detailing and joinery that she had been looking at, exemplified in the servant's attic rooms of the early seventeenth-century Queen's House in Greenwich.

Katie saw the connection, for the Shakers were émigrés who had left England for America at that precise historical moment, carrying these design patterns with them. Plain English was founded to redress this – and to do it better. Their first London showroom was in Hoxton, 'the heart of London's Shoreditch, adjacent to Spitalfields – an area which still boasts some of the finest examples of early Georgian architecture' (so says the brochure), and opened in 1995. They had thought of buying a house there and looked at many. They had walked around researching architectural details and making notes; their facsimile of an eighteenth-century china cupboard had a 'Spitalfields Hole fret-cut in the central panel for ventilation'.

A Plain English kitchen (see above) promised solid wood worktops, larders, traditional butt hinges and dovetail drawers oiled with linseed; wooden drawer slips greased with candlewax set off by ceramic sinks, dressers, farmhouse tables and country chairs; the carpentry all carried out in their workshops in Suffolk, the cabinets all painted in subfusc historical colours manufactured by another fledging company named Farrow & Ball. There were evocatively appropriate names designating town or country – Stowmarket, Wapping or Spitalfields – each styled and photographed in the 14-page brochure that I had somehow come by, more of a lifestyle design handbook than anything I had ever seen of that kind. It told me that, 'Most Plain English kitchens to date have been painted in a muted historic colour and have been fitted with old fashioned ironmongery such as brass knobs cast from worn Jacobean originals.'

This attention to historical detail and the sheer consummate perfection of their carpentry has carried on through 30 years of trading, turning Plain English into a benchmark for luxury, lifestyle and discernment, something to ogle and read about in the *How to Spend It* weekend supplements of the *Financial Times*.

Cabinetry is still manufactured in the Suffolk outbuildings of their old Georgian farmhouse, where 'it's often the re-imagining of life in this old building in its heyday – a life of genteel and bohemian aristocracy – that frames much of the inspiration for our work', their website tells us. But although I have yet to set foot in one of their showrooms, I have been tearing pages out of magazines and scrolling through their posts on Instagram and coaxing recalcitrant workmen to copy details from the original Plain English Cupboardmakers' brochure ever since, while watching their oeuvre expand, the new colour palettes and the introduction of ingenious refinements of design.

Katie told me that she 'still goes to loads of old houses and I see new things, sometimes tiny things, and I store them up.' I told her I had had five circular 'Georgian' ventilation holes punched through the very ordinary nineteenth-century four-panel doors of my kitchen cupboards and she said, 'Yes! Holes punched in cupboards, I always photograph them too.' Katie has an aversion to wall cupboards. So Plain English pioneered the concept of the full-height 'Empty Cupboard' (see bottom left) that can accommodate everything from dry goods and groceries to the fridge, a toaster kettle and en-suite breakfast bar, and waste bins and washing machines, swallowing up an entire kitchen wall and enclosing all kinds of modern or messy functionality behind plain, handsome facades and within its capacious maw. Even more beguiling is her personal fancy for making rooms within rooms using part-glazed screens to subdivide a space into different zones (see centre left), partitioning off a faux scullery, pantry or linen room, something my friend Todd Longstaffe-Gowan also accomplished 25 years ago in Stepney with old sash window frames cleverly deployed to box in the small, warmish space in which he worked. Best of all is the evocatively absurdist poetry of the strongly pigmented paint range, which trumps the wildest creative imaginings of any of their rivals, beginning gently with 'Chop', 'Kipper', 'Blancmange' and 'Jam', ascending to the glory of 'Scullery Latch', 'Starched Apron', 'Coal Scuttle', 'Dripping Tap', 'Boiled Dishcloth', 'Rice Pudding', 'Flummery', 'Silver Polish', 'Drabbled', 'Dog-Eared' and - 'Splash in a Bucket'!

For about a decade the couple also ran a little sister company, British Standard ('Simple, honest, off-the-peg wooden cupboards for your home'), a more affordable range similar to those made in the early days of Plain English (see top left). Australian chef Skye Gyngell told Katie that her British Standard kitchen had given her cooking a new lease of life when she was in a creative slump. Flattering imitations abound now. In 2013 the design site Remodelista published '10 ways to achieve the Plain English look' for which Katie prescribed range cookers made by Aga or Everhot; sinks made of ceramic, slate, copper or even concrete; floors of natural materials; old knobs, door handles and taps; and pendant light fittings or wall sconces. Versions of this look

using these elements have become ubiquitous, the virtuous normative of recycled kitchen design. And in 2021 the Shaker Style was finally routed when Plain English took their brand to America, opening a showroom in New York's Greenwich Village. *The New York Times* had already hailed the arrival of a 'new trophy kitchen' – that looked like an old one – and the romance of the larder, linking their English cachet to the success of the period TV series *Downton Abbey*. Writing about this in *The Spectator* a year later, Laura Freeman agreed, 'What the rich want now is a plain old Plain English kitchen.' As a more affordable alternative she cited a company in Somerset making 'exceptionally nice Shaker-style kitchens for St Ives fisherman's cottages and Bloomsbury basements. Boho, but bespoke.'

Katie says that they installed their first Plain English kitchen in an old Georgian house in Spitalfields in about 1995, 20 years after the pioneering days of the first squatter-settlers camping out in their slum dwellings. Although Plain English operate in a different league now, what they do and the way that they do it is demonstrably unchanged since then. And their influence has been profound. I can't ever imagine wanting a Le Corbusier-style machine for living in, but when we moved a year or so ago the idea of the kitchen was the one I puzzled over and resketched with those same torn-out pictures and that 1996 brochure open at my elbow, thinking of it as the most important room in the house to get right. I knew I didn't want one of those 'hide and seek' kitchens where every pot, bottle and modernity is hidden behind a sleek wall of cabinetry and the hunt for a cup or jar of marmalade involves opening half a dozen cupboard doors.

Flicking through my friend Charlie Hopkinson's more recent photographs in *Restoration Stories* (2019, see opposite), I'm transfixed by the modest, carefully restored Spitalfields and London-diaspora houses replete with their new–old rebuilt basement kitchens. At first glance they chime with the authentic first-phase interiors of the Spitalfields pioneers, but the quality of the joinery, the profiles of the cupboards, the treatment of counter and sink is that little bit slicker, the Quakerish make-do aesthetic of the 1970s transmuted by the knowingness of the twenty-first century. In the basement kitchen of a 1775 house in Shadwell (see opposite), the photo captions describe how 'partly glazed service cupboards run down one side of the kitchen . . . they contain a yellow-ochre walk-in pantry and wine storage room, as well as a utility room which holds the refrigeration, allowing the kitchen itself to be uncluttered'. In another house in Whitechapel, 'The kitchen design is spare . . . Round holes in the cupboard door front, as well as being decorative, allow ventilation, and small flat metal knobs give an authentic look . . . The mouldings are modest as befits a kitchen.' In yet another basement kitchen of the *c.* 1725 Spitalfields House belonging to barrister Phillip Lucas (who also deals in Georgian furniture) there is a double copper sink served by brass taps, massive oak farmhouse table, kitchen range and old kitchen dresser furnished with Delft and pewterware – the full monty. These knowing conceits – wittingly or unwittingly executed – reference an identical vocabulary, a sweet plagiarism of the Plain English style. The wheel has come full circle I think.

Part II

Making home

The house in which I was born was not very old, but it was trying to be. In a nondescript Surrey village where agriculture once eked a living from clay soils, new houses were continually arriving but politely and in low numbers. Ours was probably from just before the Second World War, its fireplaces mostly blocked up, a cold larder at the back of the kitchen, one small bathroom and diamond-leaded casement windows in a half-timbered façade. It was a second-rate example of the style christened Stockbroker's (or Mockbroker's) Tudor, its insides a tabula rasa for almost style-free living in a post-war period when money and material goods remained in short supply. There were not many pictures or ornaments, and almost nothing of my mother's, whose family home had been destroyed by wartime bombs, with everything that she owned inside.

So why then, I wonder, do I and so many of my friends live in houses full to the gunnels with really old stuff? Most of these things are not heirlooms but the spoils of 'antiquing', gathered from salerooms, eBay and car boot sales according to taste and pocket. I was born into a golden age of 'junking'. The Second World War's social and economic disruptions had radically altered the way people lived, and all over Britain, townhouses were divided up into flats, and country houses were sold, repurposed and demolished. A tsunami of strange, old, grubby and obsolete possessions – mangles and taxidermy, pot cupboards and butler's trays, chaises longues and turkey rugs – belonging to two centuries of silted-up Victorian and Georgian lifestyles poured out and submerged junk shops, street markets, country auction houses and the yards from which the rag-and-bone men still plied their trade.

I started buying old bits and bobs with pocket money at village jumble sales; progressed to the street markets of a gloriously junk-filled Brighton in my student years; and then honed my taste on anthropological safaris to the Spitalfields area of London in the early 1980s, where dedicated Fogey conservationists (see page 30) were refashioning fantasy Georgian slum life in shattered panelled rooms, with coal scuttles, candlelight and outdoor privies for their utilities.

I think there is something of a quest for personal distinction in this trait, for like works of art, objects from the pre-industrial age were handmade and so unique, granting particularity and discrimination to their owner; reputations have been built on this. And then, for those living in older houses there can be a strong sense of decorum, of doing the 'right' thing with building fabric and decoration and the furniture and pictures that enhance, fit and belong. It really is a matter of personal taste – some fetishise their pets, cars or gym habits, while others fall for a wreck or ruin that becomes their life's labour of love, a kind of religious practice. There follow the enjoyably clubby conversations about original features: lime plaster, distemper, hair plaster (one-upmanship!), cornice mouldings, the charisma of 'period' light switches and which salvage yards are still worth visiting. 'Taking a house back to how it should be' or 'rescuing' are terms I have heard so many times to describe a house purchase – or even the acquisition of something 'saved' or 'liberated' from an auction or antique shop. And afterwards, there's a great comfort to be had in surveying one's highly pleasing surroundings, like God the Father on the sixth day, when He saw what He had made, and – Behold, it was very good.

Nostalgia is dangerous. Around the time of the Millennium it seemed to be ebbing away, but things have changed again. My nostalgia takes me back to the 1970s, a time currently recalled by certain eerie revivals in fashion, hairstyles and decorating colours. Why would I want to go back to the pre-global, pre-internet era of two-bar electric fires, brown and orange carpets, shortages and keg beer? Is it because the past offers a mirage of greater innocence, lost ways of life and modes of thinking when industrial strikes, punk rock, the IRA and 'pinkos' were the most heinous threats to civil society, all homegrown and indigenous? As a fledgling curator I enthusiastically embraced the period look for a few years, hanging pictures on long cords and mocking up curtain poles out of wooden doweling. Sometimes the requirement to 'keep in period' gets a bit weird. I have friends who hide their televisions under damask cloths or in chinoiserie cabinets as devoutly as recusant Catholics sequestering a fugitive priest. Ben Pentreath remembers the 1980s' conceit of circular pedestal tables swathed in Colefax chintz à la Gervase Jackson-Stops, whose skirts, when lifted, always revealed the telly. And I am fascinated by the current phenomenon of the 'modesty apron', or pelmet – chintz, checks or stripes – so pretty and so ubiquitous, hanging in front of washing machines, sinks and dishwashers in kitchens and utility rooms. In the kitchen of our new/old house, the corpse-white faces of my white goods gleam back at me. I have bought fabric for their veiling, a block-print Indian cotton that struck me as being an original choice; maybe I'll sew them their aprons one day; maybe I'll save it for something else. And is this small rebellion a pointless dodging of the decorating zeitgeist – refusing to buy into the stock market of home decor?

My personal mantra for the descriptions of people and their houses that follow roughly seems to be that old stuff is good, and perfection is boring. So I have written about the virtuous beauty of salvage, reclamation and repurposing – particularly as found in the kitchens and bathrooms, sheds and workrooms of a large and distinguished band of my friends and acquaintances. There follows a chapter on the congruence and bohemian style and design of the domestic and studio spaces that artists and craftsmen make for themselves, and another on the old-school phenomenon that a designer friend and I have christened 'full up and classy' – the English country-house look in its myriad reincarnations. Lastly, and perhaps my favourite of all, is a celebration of the patinated antique: houses and demesnes of venerable and untrammelled antiquity with their resident populations of bats, mosses and lichens, and the Eden-like garden paradises of half a dozen or so friends, simultaneously sites of envy and beautiful repose.

Beauty, Utility, Salvage

Being a little short of money has inspired some of the nicest houses that I've known. In my north London neighbourhood in the 1980s, friends and acquaintances were living in squats and short-life housing co-ops (just as impecunious artists take studio guardianships in empty office blocks, schools and hospital buildings nowadays), practising a kind of *nostalgie de la boue*. There was a nightclub operating out of a boarded-up Chalk Farm pub, IRA protest songs and collecting buckets, and Suggs from Madness lounging on the street corner.

For a year I worked the 9 p.m. to 3 a.m. shift on the long bar at Camden's Electric Ballroom, loving its frenzied crowd-chaos and seeing all the best bands for free. When our shift ended, my friend Michael the barman and I went on to Heaven in Charing Cross in the uniforms of our respective tribes – me in black, Michael in clone-lumberjack denim – and got waved straight in, jumping the queue. It was a hand-to-mouth existence: lodgings were temporary but it was easy to find furniture, for there were rich pickings from the skips of a pre-gentrified Primrose Hill neighbourhood – club leather armchairs, cracked Victorian mirrors and a working Roberts radio in its mid-century-modern wooden case. Portobello Road's street market supplied rugs that smelt funny once brought back indoors. Back then, that frugal post-war mentality of 'make do and mend' was still embedded in our daily lives. Now that it's back in favour in the green, growing culture for recycling and vintage, I doff my hat to two of my contemporaries in particular who have kept the faith – Jane Hill and Greg Powlesland, neither of whom I knew back then, both in it for the long-term, both genius upholders of this beautiful art.

Dear Dodie
VALERIE GROVE

Shepherd's Cottage

Jane Hill

2022

My path first crossed with Jane Hill's 10 years ago, when we were both out walking our dogs. I was looking for a boy lurcher to pair with my sweet bitch, Bunny, and her Solomon and Luna were both willing and able, she said. That union was never consummated, but I saw Jane here and there, discovered that she was an art historian and could guess from the way she dressed that she was an aesthete with a strong taste for the old, beautiful and patinated. When I finally visited her ancient house, Shepherd's Cottage, I knew I was in the presence of a complete original.

Jane's house is dark and narrow, hemmed in by later, politer terraces fronting Highgate Hill. She thinks that it was first occupied by the shepherds who drove their flocks here to fatten on the open grazing grounds nearby, before taking them down to the meat markets of London. The narrow wooden staircase twists up and down between four floors, all of them filled with pictures, things, treasures. The basement kitchen with its utility scullery and sink hived off in a room at the back is especially good: cave-like, with old, scrubbed-wood surfaces, shelves and butcher's block and a settle against the wall that comfortably holds both her dear dogs – and a cat painting. Gipsy caravans and tinkers camps spring to mind – the fiery red wool blanket from a long-closed-down Welsh mill, the array of copper pans and useful metalware repurposed, tipsy oil lamps and candle sconces and a folding military-campaign chair-cum-bed. Hard wooden chairs serve as temporary filing cabinets, and the armchair swaddled in blankets by the fireplace guards three shelves of the loveliest junk-shop china, green-glazed plates and a trio of pottery owl jugs that made my covetous heart beat faster.

Via.
Jane Hill
The Cottage at 36a Highgate
London N6 5JG
PAR AVION
AIR MAIL
Period
Piece

Bonfield Block-Printers

Jane Tristram and Cameron Short

2022

Bonfield Stores was one of the oldest, handsomest shops in Thorncombe, with a dwelling house and yard behind its Fore Street shopfront. It sold fuel – charcoal, gas bottles and oil – to the surrounding neighbourhood, sinking into half-dereliction after trading ceased and then suffering a catastrophic fire. Janet Tristram and Cameron Short had spotted it a year or two before and already dreamed of making it their own. Cameron is a print maker, Janet sews, both are storytellers, and together they collaborate to produce things of magic, trading as Bonfield Block-Printers. They have stitched this badly damaged building back into a settled whole.

Simple joinery pieced together by Cameron and plasterwork are the key elements – old plaster left raw, a palimpsest of the past inhabitants, or newly made with lime. Window latches and Elizabethan embrasures, a set of casements reclaimed from a local bonfire, drab-painted matchboarding and shelves here and there, not intruding too much. Prints coming from the workshop to hang economically on drying racks above the range fireplace. Pillows, rugs, curtains and old quilts for comfort; Cameron's block-printed textiles for joy, stitched by Janet over chairs and into the linings of her beautifully fanciful Poacher's and Somerset Song coats. Mine is one of the latter, the quest that first brought me here to stand in the studio workshop for choosing and a fitting. A few days later, the end gable wall of this venerable old house, which had harboured an ominous crack, suddenly gave way and collapsed, filling this serenely beautiful room with stone dust and ancient rubble. Cameron and his father set to and rebuilt it, and less than three weeks later my new coat arrived, parcelled in brown paper, tied with twine and one perfect bird's feather.

Friederich Beck
Malmsheim
1895

JOHN NASH
BOOK DESIGNS
BARNSLEY
-SINCE 1923- MADE
Edward Barnsley and
Arts and Crafts in the Tw
Annette Carruthers

Kate Harris and Jason Goodwin

Dorset

2011–2017

I count it a lucky day that I met Kate Harris and Jason Goodwin 30 years ago at supper with mutual friends. When Kate gave me a lift home, tumbling me through the double hatch doors of their old postman's van into tinny darkness, I was completely smitten by her Mafia-style nonchalance and beauty. As the first of their four children was born, they began a sequence of moves taking them further and further off-grid, to Sussex, haute France and finally to west Dorset, where they have rooted and stuck.

Renting a succession of old farmhouses, with Kate practising her besetting talent for auction-house shopping and end-of-sale foundlings, they have made and lived in homesteads like no others, fixed in my memory – for here our children became firm friends and I passed the best of times. There's a sort of temporary wilderness of beauty in the impermanence of Kate's room arrangements. Powered by her work and will, beds and sofas come and go like stormy weather, white walls suddenly bloom into colour, then a week later every surface, each stair tread, every foot of the floor might be ankle-deep in 'stuff' like the organic bedding of a winter lambing shed. Step gingerly over an antiquarian book sans cover, a shoe, some tablemats with scenes of coaching inns and a gilded handle-less porcelain teacup. Next week, by some ergodynamic miracle, everything is calm and rehomed into a settled harmony, with new room-scapes and different pictures to look at, flowers from the garden, delicious food – and so much vivid beauty.

Tim Whittaker

Whitechapel, London

2020

The Spitalfields Trust was a beautiful invention of the 1970s, founded by militants, mavericks and anarchists to prevent London developers' wrecking balls from knocking down some of the very best residential streets at the edge of the old East End. The trust has morphed into an architectural charity that catches and purchases similarly condemned old houses in the capital and further afield, sympathetically mending and rehabilitating, and then selling them on to aesthetes and urban professionals with a taste for the past but no practical skills. For decades, Tim Whittaker was the master of this ship, steering it around the headwinds and doldrums of venture capitalists, caravan parks and the planners of London's impoverished boroughs, carrying cargoes of old stock bricks, Delft tiles, matchboarding, slate and lead.

The final project that he managed in a street near Petticoat Lane, Whitechapel, rewarded him with his own house, the last in the row, with astonishingly pretty and delicate rooms new-made inside. The invented rear staircase with its salvaged barley twist bannisters is a poem, the chimney pieces charming trouvailles, while small rooms and attics are full of borrowed light from sash windows repurposed as room dividers. All this is stitched together with darkest brown carcass furniture, dressers, octagon-glazed Georgian cupboards and cobalt-blue transfer-printed china plates.

By the summer's Sunday afternoon when I finally went to take some photographs, the house was sold, and Tim and his partner Harvey Cabaniss, former proprietor of Jeanette Winterson's famous grocery, Verde & Co, were packing up to leave. In their new place in Cumbria, a dwelling once owned by long-dead scions of the Whittaker family, they are in rustic bliss among old oak and walk across worn and sunken flags of ancient sandstone, having first dug up a carapace of cement put down by previous occupants.

MODEL: 3175/4BC
Q'TY: 1 UNIT

Belinda Eade

Shropshire

2022

The first time I was at my friend Belinda Eade's family house in Shropshire was for her wedding. The second and last, decades later, was a brief night's stay on my way south. She and her siblings were clearing the house, the mournful Proustian task of so many adult orphans on the death of their parents. Three generations of their family had lived there, and every room and outhouse was full of their once-useful, put-away things.

In the morning, while Belinda sorted her childhood into boxes, I passed through the cool subterranean chambers in the basement and then out to the stables, log sheds, apple stores and greenhouses. Under the domestic quarters were storage places, the lower corporeal organs of this dormant old house. Lined with chestnut-brown matchboarding and chill-terracotta pamment tiles lighted by dangling bulbs, were rooms for jams and bottling, for the stern business of flower arranging and the martialling of secateurs, weed-killer and trugs. Full and empty bottles had been harvested and preserved, sugary liqueurs from Christmases long past shelved next to antifreeze and methylated spirits; cardboard boxes made a strong contribution. Hooks were loaded with weather-bleached khaki outdoor gear, canvas gun and game cases flattened and voided of purpose; stout outdoor shoes, their cracked leather scraped clean, waiting on shelves high above mouse level. In the outhouses, sacks of chitterlings softened and furred with tender white sprouts. Geraniums stood sentinel in their drying pots, hopeful for their seasonal turning out of doors. Nature creeping inside, a ferny floor sprouting up between planks while spiders thickened their nets across panes of greenhouse glass.

BERRY BROS & RUDD LTD
WINE MERCHANTS
LONDON
MOËT & CHANDON
CHAMPAGNE

Gretchen Andersen

Kensington, London

2021

Gretchen Andersen followed the ebbs and flows of the antiques trade with the keen intelligence of a trawler-skipper working the seabed's teeming floor. In the fluxes of the mid-twentieth century, she had seen that the past was a foreign country full of wonderful things that no one else seemed to value. Everybody shopped at her shop, The Lacquer Chest – pop stars, Terence Conran, Elizabeth David, David Hockney, Lucian Freud. Gretchen used her sophisticated seeing eye to seek out the things that the past had discarded, always 'buying for herself', and soon her customers just wanted the things that she liked and wanted too.

Her little stuccoed house was more of a cottage, at the end of a cul-de-sac near Kensington High Street reached by a bowery path between two rows of short front gardens. It was full of wonderful things, but it's the colours and paint on the walls that I return to whenever I think of it, for hers was the palette that I held in my mind when we moved into a new-old house a couple of years ago.

Gretchen's decorating style was thrifty and self-invented, too. There were impossible-to-copy wallpapers such as the 3-shillings-a-roll marbled paper from a closing down sale, on her staircase, but I did borrow the way she'd painted the window frames and glazing bars in with the mossy green colour on the walls of her bedroom. She said that this was decorating the way the French do it and it makes the room look bigger: 'I think the English pick out everything in white.' Her knocked-through back kitchen was painted by someone she fondly described as a 'difficult genius', a colourist who used nine different yellows and then added a single muted lavender stripe to one ceiling rafter. It felt like being inside a light box, elevating the zany perfection of a red and white tin colander hanging by the sink into an art installation. Best of all was to sit on the Windsor chairs at the kitchen table for tea – and her gripping, omnivorous talk.

PREPARE

LOT
1534
All
Tack

Wormington Grange

John Evetts

2021

Where the Cotswolds segues into Gloucestershire, Wormington Grange sits on parklands at the end of a spectacularly potholed drive. I went there to write its story for *The World of Interiors* magazine, for this politely Palladian-looking country house and almost all that it contained were about to be auctioned. Purchased by an American heiress in the 1930s, the place had a late reflowering, but now its time was up – there were buckets catching rainwater all through the upper landings and a very tricky roof to repair. Wormington's last chatelain, John Evetts, had led a double life: country gent and polo player in his leisure time but also antiques finder and fixer-upper for the Landmark Trust (a charity that saves historic buildings), furnishing and furbishing up each of its new properties for as long as the trust had existed.

The stable block housed his dragon's hoard, gathered from a lifetime of criss-crossing the kingdom by van or Volvo, buying and buying and buying from antiques fairs, auctions and junk shops. In this clean, comely space built to house thoroughbreds, their grooms and carriages, oiled leather saddles made for long-dead hunters still perched along the top rails of each stall. Below were hob grates, fire irons and mahogany boot racks, piles of madder rose-pink turkey carpets, thickets of chairs, myriad looking glasses and picture frames and older and weirder things that I couldn't identify or desperately coveted. John was justly proud of all this plunder gathered in a worthy cause, the mountain of turned wooden towel rails a symbolic *nunc dimittis* that completed his furnishing of each Landmark Trust folly, cottage or castle he had fitted out. The auction-house people were already tying on labels with their lot numbers. Two months later, on the day of the sale, not one of my hopefully placed bids came good.

Mallets Cottage

Matthew Rice and David Wherrett

2024

Matthew Rice and David Wherrett collect what is broadly classified as Folk Art. For 19 years they had a 'never dry', always damp net loft in St Ives, Cornwall, and it was there that they came across the marine artist Alfred Wallis. 'He was the entry, he was also an introduction to the primitive or the not taught – that felt significant at the time,' says Matthew. After a while, Matthew couldn't stop buying primitive stick-back chairs, and so this little old house in Suffolk that's part medieval and part Elizabethan has become a sort of shrine and tabernacle for their collection. In the seventeenth century it had served as the village workhouse. We hope it was a nice workhouse, they say. It is redeemed now in any case, for what goes on here now is a beautiful labour of love.

David, who works for the NHS by day, ploughs and scatters every weekend on the field-cum-allotment garden that stretches out behind the house. There is a pleasing Beatrix Potter order and fecundity to everything he does in the horticultural line; his fingers are the greenest, his cottage garden is blousy, cluttered and expressive. 'I was sort of pottering from very early on,' he remembers. They put the house right, unpicking recent modernisations, painting it in calm, drab earthy colours, and putting back casement windows. Finding a whole floor from a medieval building that was being removed, they bought it and used it to face the new partition walls, coaxing their builders to abandon professional perfectionism for a more rough-and-ready finish that would blend old work and new, some of which they admit was a bit 'bonkers'. They put up with the house's narrow staircases and small windows.

Maybe the kitchen is the most perfect room of all in its utility and order. There's a washing machine and dishwasher but they are 'nicely hidden away', the floor is laid with old Norfolk pamments and everything else, except the Aga is handmade. All the things you see are in use: the wooden spoons and cider mugs, cow creamers, candle prickets, stick-back chairs and the exquisite patchwork counterpanes on the beds. Agnes, their darling French bulldog, laps water from a Delftware bowl and rests in a box-bed of ancient oak. On the top of a bedroom corner cupboard, lucky black cats with button eyes are the household gods in their lararium.

The Bothies

Ben Pentreath and Charlie McCormick

2021–2024

The weather comes in fast on the west coast of Scotland. Ben Pentreath and Charlie McCormick's twin bothies stand loch-side and shoulder to shoulder, fed by spring water, heated by fire; a green eco-dream with an outdoor compostable lavatory. They fill up a tin hip bath with jugs from two large village hall-style tea urns. 'On a cold, dark winter's evening you just go to bed,' they say.

When they came here, the older of these dwellings was ruined and roofless, and the other, dating from the 1890s, had been empty for nearly 50 years. The first is now the room of all utilities, with a cement floor poured straight onto bare earth and an insulated ceiling made of railway sleepers. Things from their Dorset life (see page 219) have moved here with them: kitchen ceramics from the pound stall in Bridport market; Charlie's dresser from the Old Parsonage's flower room that he painted blue and then bright red. Now in conker brown it looks appropriately Scottish Presbyterian. The other bothy has two matchboarded dwelling rooms for sitting and sleeping, brown furniture, tartan rugs, Staffordshire pottery, flowered chintz that is washable when the dogs jump muddily onto it. Books and naval charts that belonged to Ben's father. It's cottage hardcore – a cup of tea means a trip to the well-spring with buckets, but the log man delivers.

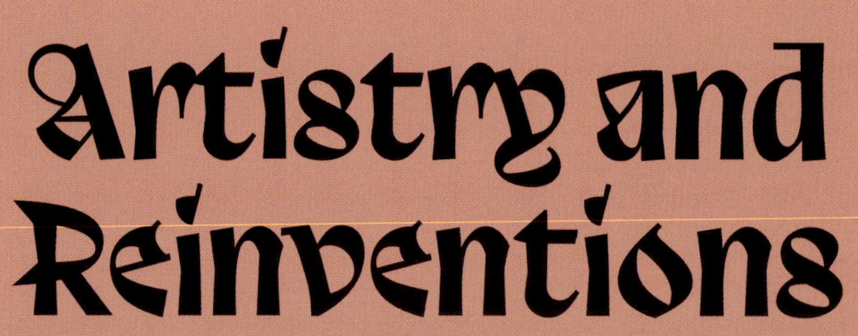
Artistry and
Reinventions

So many books have been written about artists' houses; the terms 'studio', 'bohemian' and 'aesthete' overstretched and reworked to describe the way in which Ben Nicholson and Barbara Hepworth matched white walls with squares and angles, the Bloomsbury Group painted tabletops for tablecloths and fired their own earthen dinner services, the acid-trip-patterned surround of setting up home with a pre-Raphaelite Brother, the outré clothes they chose to wear.

It is true that 'arty' people may feel compelled to extend their practice and present themselves ready-curated and public-facing, turning life into art and art into life, and this is why the rest of us like to keep an eye on what they do with a view to possible acts of plagiarism – for imitation is the highest form of flattery, as they say. If you've got an eye for the harmony and settled, unifying composition of a half-decent work of art, maybe you want to find that reflected back in your studio pottery mug or Chinese-export porcelain cup of milkless Lapsang. And artists tend to surround themselves with very lovely things, vernacular and folk arts and crafts, old textiles and prints, handmade pottery, old glass and silver. Clothing of choice is very often 'old', vintage or vintage-looking too, made of 'honest' materials – hemp and linen, velvets and silk – fashioned on the patterns of past working lives; the baggy chore jacket and the faux-fisherman's Breton T-shirt, variations of the cropped matelot trouser, the clever siren-styling of the Toast catalogue. Like this, everything everyday can be all of a piece, unity by inclusion; the humbler utilitarian goods enhanced by their proximity as the props to high-status art, the art works serene and untroubled by the incursions of jarring, potentially 'ugly' modernity.

But this is only what we, the imitators, can achieve: everyday life *imitating* the higher, arty life. In the houses that follow, the hod-carrying work of real artists is taking place. Their inhabitants get up early; mix paint or model clay, wax or papier-mâché; cut patterns or shape wire and wood; inhale fumes; dirty their clothes and surroundings; and push things about to clear more space in which to work. David Gentleman requires a perfect order in his top-floor studio, a calm formalist precision of tools, brushes and cleared surfaces. Viola Lanari has spare and tranquil rooms for living in and a full-up studio on the other side of town that is all stations go. Romi Behrens and Rose Hilton practised a sweet disorder that flowed across into their casually appointed living rooms, something Rose's friend the poet W.S. Graham called 'the beat style'. Peter Hone styles *everything* – his breakfast settings, his plate rack, his pyjamas, the bathroom walls. Janet and Cameron at Bonfield Block-Printers raise three daughters whose bedrooms give the nod to their youthful preferences without falling out of step with the old house's manners. And Mark Hearld is an omnivore, a tireless maker, worker and consumer of everything that's old, original and authentic.

MOVING
PRINTING WITH SPIRIT
Mary Fedden
Michael Rothenstein
Mary Newcomb
Barbara Jones
Winifred Nicholson
Enid Marx
David Hockney
Peter Blake
Vanessa Bell
Elizabeth Frink
Ceri Richards

Mark Hearld

York

2021

On a road trip to the far west coast of Scotland, via Edinburgh and the Black Isle, the first leg was by train, so I arranged to get out at York to visit the house of artist and maker Mark Hearld, near the city's old medieval walls. I guessed his front door from its distinctive brass fox-mask knocker that was weathering to a witchy viridian green. The only thing to say when you go into Mark's house is 'Blimey!' and 'Blimey!' again and again. It has very fine bones, Regency going backwards and forwards from this high point in architectural aspiration, and original paint on the walls of the long narrow hallway that is the colour of rust and blood.

Mark impulsively buys anything and everything that was made by non-industrial processes: fairground art and shop signage; prints and pottery; *objets trouvés* and taxidermy; vintage costume; the nice and the beautiful (he is a very natty dresser). He makes and curates work that fits around this beautiful thesis, and there is a unity by inclusion in the way he lives among all these items and his own signature pieces silt down and cross-pollinate with the work of so many other hands.

24

David and Sue Gentleman

London

2024

For a life of contrasts, there's artist and designer David Gentleman, who was my neighbour for a couple of decades in one of the boskier streets of Camden Town. David had trained at the Royal College of Art, where Edward Bawden, John Nash and Kenneth Rowntree taught him in the 1950s. He was often to be found out of doors sketching passing street- and wild-life: skinny youths in hoodies waiting for their man; urban dogs snuffling and micturating; bag-laden shoppers hurrying home from Marks & Spencer's food hall. Once or twice we had a half-pint together in the pub at the top of Delancey Street, where Dylan Thomas briefly lived and (no doubt) drank his deep potations, and David and his wife, Sue, generously allowed me to record the cool understated rooms of their family home, one of the calmest I know.

Sue arranged this tall, terraced house more than 40 years ago and the sensibilities of this married pair chime closely, for there is a complementary completeness in the way in which David's work belongs in Sue's airy interior spaces. Lines and angles are clean cut, and colours are pure and clear; a shared visual intelligence and humour governs all of it. David's campaigning posters for the National Trust march along the hall and stairs, his wood blocks fill a vitrine on the top landing. 'Artists are people who design things,' he says. Symmetry prevails in spaces and white space, and there are clever, unconventional installations: a giant shell on a midget chair; a rocking horse over-door; a sculpturally fluid bentwood rocking chair pinned above the deep void of the stairwell.

David's drawing studio on the top floor has the same clean, scrupulous sense of order as the engine house that is the basement kitchen. His rows of drawing impedimenta and pinboard sketches march to the same beat as the grisaille chinaware ranged down there on triple shelves. One is an alphabet plate by Eric Ravilious, two are the Covent Garden tankard mugs that David designed for stylist and fellow designer David Mellor.

This house had been renovated for its previous owner by the architect John Prizeman, its basement kitchen making the front cover of a Design Council handbook in the 1960s. As David and Sue could afford to change very little and didn't much want to, the basement kitchen is still there. In the bathroom, the William Morris willow-patterned wallpaper that they put up in the 1970s brings the treetops outside, inside. In 2003 David designed march placards for the Stop the War Coalition, a bloodstain motif with the single short word 'NO', a poster with the brilliant visual economy of a postage stamp. It is a rare gift to be able to think so cogently in words and images.

Frenchmans Creek

Greg Powlesland

2022

Lots of people down my end of Cornwall know Greg Powlesland, but I can't remember how we met. For a year or two I badgered him, asking to photograph his place, and after quite some time he conceded that I might. I knew he was boaty, for I had taken him to meet my friend Michael Johnson of the Newlyn Copperworks and in return he had asked us to a party he was having at his hidden-away boathouse on the Helford River. This was to christen the new quay he had built of granite reclaimed from a tin-mine engine house and a little hand-built clinker boat that was ceremonially launched that night and rowed up and down.

Greg is an artist, sculptor, maker, teacher, builder, restorer and salvager of the highest order. He works to the highest standard – but he has the skills of architect, engineer, boat builder, metal worker and sail maker to boot. In the lofty top-lit studio that he designed and built onto his boat-shed, there are zones for everything, including a drawing table and the sewing table that's a repurposed 2-metre- (7-foot-) long dining table of yew, rosewood and ebony he made when he was teaching at the John Makepeace School at Parnham House. But most extraordinary of all is his tool cupboard of pine and yew made at Parnham, its plain exterior disguised in a pretty, pale blue primer that he picked up at the local builder's yard. His students were hanging their tools on plywood, so he told them: if you're going to make exquisite furniture, you need to present yourself properly.

Everything is made to the same benchmark of excellence, and Greg's wardrobe of work clothes performs the same marriage of beauty with utility and decorum. He had made a wonderful denim smock once with the sail maker's sewing machine that he got from an old sail wright in Wivenhoe, but then he lost it. Greg finds whatever else he needs by swapping things with other kindred spirits. The story he told me that I like best of all is this one:

I had an old hay wain – there was a wheelwright in Colyton in Devon, and I went to see him about restoring the wheels. He had this saw in his workshop from the 1880s, it does everything a modern saw will do. So, we did a trade, and I got the saw and a little woodstove. He got the hay wain, he restored it. It's the one that was used in the film Far from the Madding Crowd.

ARMSTEAD

Crowland Manor

Sophie Wilson
2024

When I finally got to Crowland Manor, Sophie Wilson was already poised for a flight into Dorset and a different life there with her young children. Her house – built in the sixteenth century and almost every century afterwards, and substantially enlarged in 1690 – was as strange and extraordinary as the Fenlands that girdle it, with the same strong spirit of place and ancient permanence.

It's the colours that stop you first, the sheer breadth and depth of sub-arsenic, slub green and raspberry-russet ochre-pink that rushes through all the passageways and up the twisting dog-leg staircase. Colour goes everywhere: above and below dado rails; into china cupboards and across shutters, doors and glazing bars; and up to the cornice, a beautiful smothering and coddling effect. Add to that the conker brown and the patina produced by smoky age and solid fuel to keep you from freezing in winter; and an ink-blue downstairs bathroom with a shower curtain of verdure tapestry.

Sophie's delicate sgraffito slipware ceramics sold through her 1690 store were lined up waiting in drill-yard perfection for their firing. There were some fired and finished jugs in the kiln-cum-laundry room on the other side of the house, spikey and exotic, referencing Chinese export imari wares but wholly themselves. Then I began noticing everything else: the superb textile of a heavy door curtain; the slip-cover on the armchair pulled up next to the kitchen range; that cushion on a chair on the half-landing, scraps of archive designs by Schumacher, Liberty and Collier Campbell. Their patterns – delicate, historicising, vegetable – and the selective tones of red, blue, green, brown and a soft grey that I kept finding and appreciating come from the same colour library that Sophie references as a ceramicist. Her ex had wanted to re-create a museum house of the seventeenth century, but Sophie just wanted this house to stay as it was, to make the sort of home she might have visited as a kid: 'the softness of that before technology took over. The house and the work is a seamless thing for me,' she said, 'and it always has been. The work that I produce is for the house.' This is the mark of true artistry, an Artist's House.

Alan Dodd

Islington, London

2011–2020

Alan Dodd is a very natty dresser, with a capacious wardrobe of beautiful sports jackets, corduroys and neckerchiefs that are more or less cravats. His clothes make me think of gunsmiths, Lord's Cricket Ground and the Cavalry Club, but he has never been known to take an iota of interest in any such establishments. Recently on his Instagram account, Alan posted a picture of an extraordinarily desirable pink cotton damask shirt, which he had run up on his grandfather's 1898 Singer sewing machine and worn on New Year's Eve in 1966. He had sewn a matching mini-dress for his then girlfriend too. Since he had outgrown the shirt, I asked if I could have it, but he said no.

Which is all a preamble, leading up to Dodd's lifelong avocation as a painter and muralist of high regard. His painting store and studio in Islington doubles as his dressing room, with suit bags slung from the wardrobe and rolled-up canvases on top and below, a batterie of ivory hairbrushes and a crowded work table featuring a red telephone that no longer rings. Alan went to Maidstone College of Art (where Hockney was one of his teachers) and the Royal Academy schools, and hung out with painter friends who had formed The Broadleaf Brotherhood, a precursor of the Brotherhood of Ruralists. A few paintings from his 'Magic Realism' phase are hanging about on the staircase here, his acid-trip-wonderful masterpiece is a painting of Fonthill Abbey done in 1974 (see page 187), which, so far, he refuses to sell.

Domestic bondage and the distaff side

Perhaps women go about making a house differently? For so many *femmes sérieuses* there is conflict in the responsibility to make a home while following a life that is intellectually and creatively viable. My mother's generation had far fewer choices, while my own life has encompassed much greater freedoms and opportunities than hers. Rachel Cusk noticed that the novelist and philosopher Iris Murdoch was famous for living in sensational domestic squalor, that her refusal of a domestic role probably needed to be 'louder and more emphatic than most people's' in Oxford's male-dominated academe. Yet, between mess and mould and huge productivity, Murdoch was not immune to 'thing envy', the kind of covetousness promulgated by the *Financial Times' How to Spend It* supplement. She used her royalties to buy a tiny painting by Samuel Palmer, an Elizabethan tapestry and a generously proportioned eighteenth-century house in a pretty Cotswolds village.

I thought about this again last week at Rosudgeon car boot sale when I bought a copy of *Housewife* magazine published in 1951 at a pricey 1 shilling and 6 pence. Its pages catered for the bondage of a 1950s domestic goddess, with glamour tips and impossible aspirations, receipts to woo a curmudgeonly husband, 'family' menus and inventive ways with soft furnishings. A writing competition, 'I dreamed I had £30 and this is how I spent it', suggested, 'If you won £30 you would probably spend it on new curtains.' For many women coming of age in post-war Britain, motherhood meant a breaking off of the intellectual or creative life or a doubling of roles, with the domestic invariably trumping the creative and the impossibility of corralling that thing rated essential by Virginia Woolf, 'A Room of One's Own' (see page 23). I can think of many such women who kept a vocation on a low simmer while all this was going on, then threw themselves into the business of making art full time again in the sudden luxury of time and space reclaimed in later life. For others, faced with the prospect of dwindling into compromise or mediocrity, the pilot light flickered and simply went out.

Prussia Cove

Romi Behrens

2017

Among the former was Romi Behrens, a legendary character in her far-flung kingdom of west Cornwall. I only met her in the last few years of life, yet her ebullient, zestful spontaneity meant that our friendship galloped along. She liked to show and tell, and the old dower house-farmhouse that she was living in was as full up with her paintings as the barns enclosing its courtyard. After becoming a farmer's wife in the unemancipated 1960s, this clever educated young woman fixed on painting as the 'something for myself' that could maintain her sense of identity. She'd made a painting a day, she told me, and had remained obstinately deaf to the entreaties of many of those who'd clamoured to buy them. She hung her own work unselfconsciously on every wall and cottage windowsill – pictures were stacked on floors and in cardboard boxes in the bedrooms and ranged around and above her own double bed. Her subjects were close to home and its spirit of place: a bowl of potatoes, a John Dory, the dogs, almost everyone she met in her omnivorous daily life, and the roofscapes, cottage ends and contours of places nearby.

Shopping in a local warehouse, I glanced upwards and spotted a couple of Romi's paintings, skied under ceiling girders, the portraits of its long-dead proprietor and one of the shelf-stackers. She had little interest in material things and no idea of the value of money – stabbing in the dark at a figure of '£20,000 AT LEAST!' for one of her best paintings. She might agree to a sale then maddeningly change her mind – and actually stole one picture back. To Romi, selling pictures merely confirmed her unshakeable belief in her work – 'Isn't that AMAZING?' and 'Look at THIS one!' She was genius at tabletop still-life, panettone boxes and birthday cakes.

Rose Hilton

Botallack, Cornwall

2010 - 2016

Rose Hilton's life was a complicated one played out in three parts. Born in Kent, into a large family who were members of the fundamentalist Plymouth Brethren sect, her determined character got her to a local art college, then to a London one, culminating in a place at the Royal College of Art, where she won a prestigious Prix de Rome scholarship. Then in 1958, the painter Sandra Blow introduced her to the much older Roger Hilton, a clever, maverick, more established artist and a drinker. During their on-off love affair, Rose had a child, and the pair eventually set up house together in remote west Cornwall.

Their house was a terrace of three small miners' cottages built from local granite blocks and rubble, with wide views across compartmented fields, close to the tin workings whose shafts fissure the land and tunnel beneath the sea here. It housed a few miscellaneous antiques of Roger's. 'I suppose we just got the rest from second-hand shops,' Rose told me. 'I was still a student at heart, but I think if you're an artist you're visual, so you usually paint walls white and have flowers and nice materials.' The house was full of paintings, including the rampant nude Roger frescoed onto the newly plastered wall outside the bathroom, hidden for some years afterwards behind a new boiler. When their friend the poet Sydney Graham arrived to look over what they had done, he privately observed, 'Rose has the beat style.' Here on Roger's insistence, Rose had given up painting for a *bouleverse* life as his wife, the mother of his two sons and then as his nurse in the bedridden years before his death in the 1970s. The experience marked her but phoenix-like: she returned to painting and 40 years more of loves and friendships, pleasures and a kind of 'functional' drinking that was one of the legacies of her marriage.

Rose liked her house and the things in it – the conservatory she had added with its tangles of leggy geraniums – but she was never house proud. She painted at first in a room upstairs, then took on a sequence of studios in Penzance and Newlyn to which she commuted every day. 'When you are painting you have to throw yourself into it. You have to think it all the time. Go to bed early. You can't just go up and do a bit and come down again. It's a whole way of life. You need to concentrate on the work and look at it a lot too.' The paintings here, which are among her best, were photographed in her Newlyn studio in 2012. Her painting came back to her and her house looked after itself.

Prue Piper

Marston Bigot, Somerset

2015–2022

Prue Piper lives in an exhilaration of wind. Her dwelling in Somerset was once the old laundry and drying room for a neighbouring 'big house', set near the top of a slope where washing lines flapped in the line of duty. Vegetables grow now where linen sheets billowed and tugged at their pegs. It's where Prue and her late husband, Edmund Piper, brought up their children, and it has always been a house of art. Edmund painted, photographed and designed pyrotechnical firework displays with his father, the neo-Romantic painter John Piper. He co-authored the Shell county guides and specialised in cross-genre black and white photographs too, which combined landscape, heritage-architecture and erotic nudes, often with Prue as his model (*Nudes*, Old Laundry Press, 2000).

Being highly practical, with a doctorate in Biochemistry, Prue adapted herself, chameleon-like, attending local pottery classes and then teaching herself the rest, equipped with the kiln from John Piper's Fawley Bottom studio. Her own studio now occupies the coal stores that powered the Victorian laundry here and were next repurposed as her children's bedrooms. Her plates and mugs and Staffordshire-like figurines of Celtic gods and green men, frogs and birds, are like nobody else's. Her son Henry and his family live in the other half of the house, harvesting all their electricity from the wind's power, which sends the kinetic sculptures he makes from scrap metal and salvage whirling outside.

THE
OLD

Ann Stokes

Hampstead, London

2011

And Ann Stokes! Whose ceramics were just like her, extravagant and lively and made with an experimental, spontaneous hand. Her work is probably more unorthodox, more idiosyncratic and more free than any of her generation; happily now a host of younger potters such as Rose de Borman are making pieces that she'd appreciate. When I met her she was in her Tree phase, and these fragile constructions that her son had wired for sound had taken over the entire ground floor of her old house in Hampstead's Church Row – squirrels, owls and songbirds festooned their branches – twittering and hooting to me. She'd begun potting in the 50s and gained a celebrity following – the decorator John Fowler commissioned giant planters from her for his country folly, The Hunting Lodge. Unimpressed by Fowler, her staircase hall was painted a shrieking grass green he'd never have countenanced, a foil to a polychrome stair carpet she'd made with the tonal punch of a painting by Patrick Heron. Her life's trajectory had been as unconventional as her art, at 17 she'd gone to live with her elder sister Margaret Mellis and her husband Adrian Stokes, joining the artists colony in Carbis Bay in St. Ives, then becoming Stokes's second, child-wife. In middle age she'd married again and found her own vocation, making a Noah's Ark's worth of zoomorphic pieces, life-sized crocodiles, fountains, looking glasses, tiles and many many vessels for eating and drinking. She gave me a piece of birthday cake at her kitchen table. It was his birthday cake, her husband the Orwell scholar Ian Angus told me, and he'd just gone out to buy it, for she had completely forgotten the significance of the day, he added fondly.

DIY

Nell Lyhne

Westbourne Grove, London

2023

A new friend, made remotely during the miseries of the pandemic and now a firm, physical fact of my life, is Nell Lyhne: painter, architect and much more besides. Sixteen years ago, finding herself cash-strapped and single with four children, she moved them into the basement and ground floor of a Victorian terraced house near Westbourne Grove and addressed herself to making a home there. She calls this an essay in stuffing everyone in and making every square inch work very hard.

Nell made a kitchen in the largest front room, with its huge bay window. The logic should have been white paint everywhere, but instead she opted for the ombré of Farrow & Ball's grey-black Down Pipe. At first they hated it, but with no splashbacks or tiling there's a serendipity in just touching it up whenever it looks shabby. The bookcase cupboard is a larder, the cushion on the Lloyd Loom chair is an exquisite fragment of verdure tapestry, the copper *batterie de cuisine* gleams out of Caravaggio-esque shadow. In the tiny sitting room, butter-yellow paint knits everything together, assimilating a nineteenth-century cast-iron fire surround that Nell picked up off the street outside. Swagged curtains are of vintage glazed chintz by Mrs Munro, the ceiling is a rich Prussian blue, a curing leg of Serrano ham hangs among drying laundry. Nell's basement painting studio is a room where paint is spilt, colour mixed and brushes cleaned on the plaster walls. It's home, although the practical and aesthetic constraints of life here have been 'interesting' ones, she finds.

Peter Hone

Notting Hill, London
2018

Peter Hone is a master-plaster-caster, the only one of his kind. People dropped in at his studio flat on the piano nobile of a Notting Hill townhouse all the time, to goggle at him, try to buy things from him and – like me – to take photographs. In a life of contrasts he has worked at the zoo; as a custodian in peaked cap and silver buttons at the Banqueting House, the Jewel Tower and Chiswick House; as antiques dealer in residence for Lord Rothschild's fabled Clifton Nurseries; and now as a top-rate fabricator in plaster and resin. He sometimes claims that he was a foundling, left in a basket, raised in an orphanage in Rochdale. 'I was born wonderful,' he adds.

Periodically, Peter calls in the auction houses, has a clear out, sells everything and starts again. He got the lovely shell pink on his slip-covers by washing them with an old crimson velvet cushion. He guards the secrets of his techniques but recently succeeded against all expectations in casting giant *Gunnera* leaves in plaster. When he visited us in Lamorna Cove he lost no time in commanding Jack Chauncy to wade thigh-deep in the little stream that gushes into the sea there, to harvest him a fresh crop. Peter claims to have the bikini worn by Camilla Parker Bowles as a girl, which he obtained from her then neighbours, the Edens secreted in a cupboard. Sometimes he says he'll let me see it, sometimes he says he won't.

CHARLES I

Viola Lanari

West Brompton, London

2021

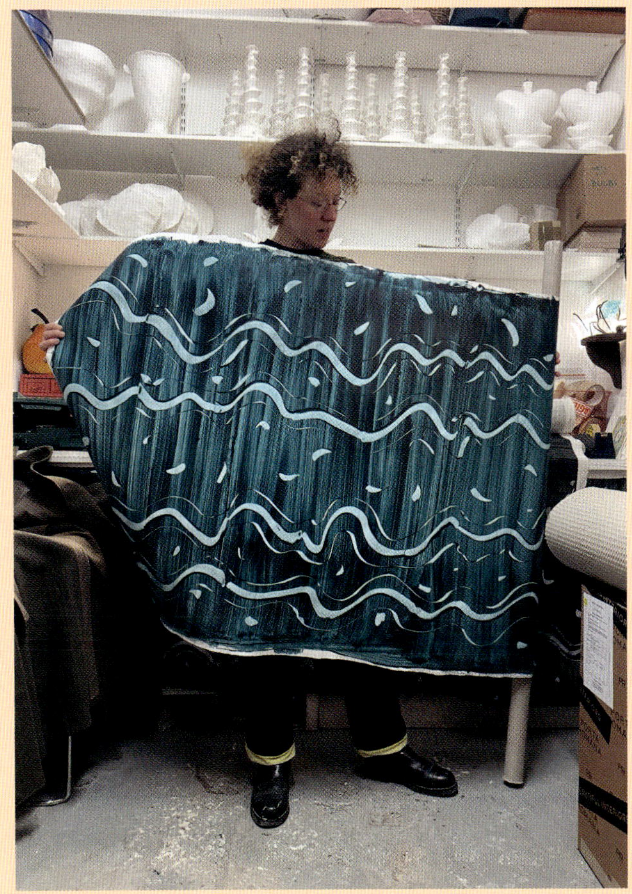

'I am British now, I've never been Italian in Italy. Today I just finished my second jar of Marmite. So, I am bloody English!' says Viola Lanari, self-invented, self-taught maker of unique, idiosyncratic things. She works mostly in plaster, devising and perfecting her own methods. Born in Milan into an Anglophile family, Viola was always trying to get to England, taking a course at Central Saint Martins, then a degree in Philosophy, which she hated. She is funny, vivid and knows how to get the best out of life. At college she found she was good at drawings and 'little stories', so she sent a desperate plea to the creative team at *The World of Interiors* and started a series of temporary placements there that took her to the happier place she inhabits now.

Lamps started Viola off, as did the business of transforming the lacklustre fittings in her West Brompton flat – where she made an extraordinarily organic console table, like something for a disco-Greco cave dweller, for a spot just inside the door. She taught herself little by little, managing the plaster's quick chemical reactions. 'You cannot mess around. I'm still learning.' She has a silver vinyl-papered hallway ('Debo Devonshire, a posh person, had silver in her bathroom, I saw it in *Interiors*') and a silver ceiling insulating her studio, to keep back the mice. Here she makes expressive lamps that are like flowers, picture frames and chunky sculpted pieces inspired by Picasso and Brancusi – 'like medieval furniture', building the material up in careful layers, moulding scrim or working over metal armatures, carving and patinating, designing fabric and papers for shades and furnishing. Her taste and preferences are, *au fond*, informed only by herself, and all the better for that.

Bridie Hall

De Beauvoir Town, London

2020

With the purest, most exacting vision of all my friends, the artist designer Bridie Hall ran away from New Zealand after finishing art school, to seek her fortune in London (a reverse migration, for her maternal grandmother had been an English war-bride). She is a shopkeeper too, partner and co-owner of Pentreath & Hall, after a serendipitous meeting 20 years ago when she was working for designer Thomas Heatherwick. She had cast him a little waxed, ebonised plinth for his birthday. Someone asked, 'Who made this?' She said, 'I did!' and they went outside for a cigarette. This was Ben Pentreath, newly arrived from a stint working in New York. They kept in touch, he called in at her house in Columbia Road, Hackney, and always wanted to see what Bridie was making there. One day she was painting William Smalley's Rugby Street bathroom silver – which it still is – and Ben came in and said – 'I've got this SHOP! Do you want to run it?'

When she was renovating her old house in De Beauvoir Town in Hackney, north London, Bridie made a 'drawing' room off the kitchen, with a birch-ply work table designed by William Smalley, and shelves and walls covered with sketches for ideas and designs in progress. But her major spheres of influence are her work rooms in Pentreath & Hall's huge studio workshop near Grays Inn Road in Holborn. She told me that in New Zealand, because they were so far away from the rest of the world, there were few imports but instead a great deal of ingenuity and making it yourself. Her dad had a copy of The Complete Book of Self-Sufficiency, The Classic Guide for Realists and Dreamers by John Seymour (1976). 'I've got a copy too.' She is skilled at all kinds of decorative paint finishes, decoupage and potichomania, ceramics and stitch craft, modelling, casting and plasterwork. Bridie's latest masterpieces are the soap-cake intaglio cameos that she has invented featuring classical Roman heads. Her tastes are eclectic and original, and she is an inventor of genius – while remaining wholly matter of fact.

INSPIRATION
ODILON REDON

Westlab
Westlab
PINK GIN

Full up and Classy

My friend the interior decorator Daniel Slowik and I shared a joke that lasted for two or three years. It's not particularly funny and doesn't happen so much now, but we've both enjoyed typing the single comment 'classy' under each other's Instagram posts and occasionally on those of others. It's never pejorative, but it does work best when Daniel says it out loud, enunciated in a tone that reminds me of the comic actor Terry-Thomas. It's an accolade of approval although it doesn't designate anything very specific.

A few years ago we still lived in a tall house in a terrace on the north side of Regent's Park, the 'wrong' side of the park as it would have been known when these houses were being built. Once sooty and now grubby Camden Town marched alongside our street, and the Euston mainline railway surged by on the other side, impossible to ignore even as a new band of young estate agents had begun marketing this area to credulous buyers as a hitherto secret annex of Primrose Hill. I'd quite liked this house but never loved it, there was something not quite friendly about its gaunt architectonic spaces. There was only one room with which I felt fully content and that was nothing special, a first-floor drawing room that I protected from dogs and children, equipped with a drinks tray and a few cushions, pictures and bits of china I prized the most. There was a working marble fireplace and an old two-bar electric fire (see page 241) for when we couldn't be bothered, very like the one that the late Queen posed with for a casual photograph in 1967. I would sometimes sit here briefly feeling calm because there was nothing terribly wrong in eyeshot that seemed to demand an immediate style intervention. It wasn't grand, but I hoped that it might understudy for the accolade 'classy'.

But all the rooms in all the houses that follow deserve to be honoured with this term. They are all different, some have been in situ for decades and some only a few years, but they are all here because they are rather more than quotidian, aspiring to something of a higher order. None were put together by minimalists, and many have distinguished pedigrees. The writer Anthony Powell collaged and decorated the rooms in his Regency-era house in Somerset as a panacea in interludes of insomnia or writer's block, choosing extraordinary wallpapers and rich velvety colours. Sculpture expert and collector David Bridgwater decorated very little but filled up the rooms of his Bath townhouse with a choice miscellany of the rarest most unusual things he had ever found. Domenica More Gordon's artist mother invented a whole new school of exquisite decoration out of *necessitas* in her local Scottish salvage yard and with her textile and sewing skills. Ben Pentreath cut his teeth as a decorator in the perfectly proportioned rooms of an old parsonage in Dorset and then carried on his life there with his partner Charlie McCormick's exuberantly casual embellishments and accretions. Jane MacEwan and Min Hogg made everything around them look effortlessly right and uniquely unlike but better than the rooms lived in by anyone else. I've admired all the houses that follow for sharing something of this distinguished, unstudied approach to the making of home.

Domenica More Gordon

Edinburgh

2015–2016

After a stint working in Los Angeles, Domenica More Gordon and her husband, Charlie Fletcher, brought their young children back home, to her family house a few miles north of Edinburgh. Domenica's parents were artists, and they had found this austerely beautiful eighteenth-century sandstone house in the 1980s in a run-down state. Her father, Harry, taught at the Edinburgh Art School and had also been a designer on Vogue magazine, he loved painting portraits, flamboyant patterns and oriental fabrics. Her mother, Marianne, who trained at the Central School of Art & Design, is a maker in textiles and three dimensions, and a genius at junk-shop furnishings.

'This house is all about Mum and family and roots,' Domenica told me. Marianne's aqueous colours and patterns suffuse the rooms, but she used strong colour too, the crimson four-poster in the green panelled bedroom is hung with an antique linen found at a local junk yard that she had painstakingly washed and restored; my guest bedroom was full of her exquisite textiles and frilled bed linens.

I'd met Charlie and Domenica years earlier, holidaying with a gang of mutual friends in the Outer Hebrides, and although I was delighted by them both, Domenica was far too modest then ever to reveal what it was she did. In fact, she is an artist, illustrator and textile designer, a graduate of Central Saint Martins who worked out of a studio in the corner pavilion of the house's courtyard, designing and making the anthropomorphically wonderful dogs and animals sculpted from felted wool that feature in her children's books and stories too. 'I chose dogs because they are such good channels of emotion,' she says. Each collection she made was unique, some fully kitted out in astonishing bonsai historical wardrobes. They have a sweet, toy-like quality; the smallest fit in the palm of your hand. They were bought by collectors worldwide and sold through the Arts & Science craft and maker shops in Japan.

David and Sarah Bridgewater

Bath

2017

David Bridgwater sent me a mysterious message, referencing our shared interest in classical sculpture and suggesting I should see his house, a weird blind date that turned out beautifully. The house stands in one of the grander streets of early Georgian Bath and was chock-a-block with David's extraordinary trouvailles. Antique dealers' houses often incite the greatest envy in me, for the most discerning truffle out things that you and I will never get a whiff of and live among them in princely disarray, until the fascination has worn off or they decide to liquidate some assets and fund the purchase of something even more fabulous. Parts of David's house were as densely packed as Sir John Soane's Museum in London's Lincoln's Inn Fields, but calmer and set off by pale dove-grey walls; the fun here was that we could pick everything up. David is a scholar with a profound interest in the provenance of all the objects he buys. 'I bought my first bust of Alexander Pope back in 2000. I went to the V&A. They said, "Oh, it's nineteenth century, there's hundreds of them." I found an engraving of it from 1788, it couldn't have been any other bust. It was by Roubiliac.'

David and his wife, Sarah, brought this handsome place back into domestic use after a period when it had been used as offices and fitted throughout with strip lights. They kept just one in the huge kitchen, where each bit of furniture stood 3 metres (10 feet) apart from the others. David's ground-floor study was his treasure house, packed like a pharaoh's tomb of miscellanea – a Bidriware hookah pipe, a Renaissance portrait tondo. Another smaller room could only be described as a 'cabinet of curiosities'. Behind some Victorian curtain poles and a toothy cross-cut saw was a papier-mâché overmantel panel with a frieze of hounds chasing a fox in pursuit of a hare. It wasn't perfect, someone had tried to clean it with paint stripper, but David had carefully picked off the rest of the overpaint himself. A year or so later, after thinking of the panel almost every day, I finally bought it from David, and last week it was married into the reinstated chimneypiece in the room where I'm writing this.

P.L.W.P.

Divan Japonais
CHILDREN'S BOOKS
FOR SALE HERE

The Chantry

Anthony Powell
2017

I read Anthony Powell's novel sequence, *A Dance to the Music of Time* (1951–1975), in my thirties. I think that's a good age to fall into this epic saga of love, life and suffering (which was begun soon after publication of his crony Evelyn Waugh's *Brideshead Revisited* in 1945), when one becomes more capable of a Proustian empathy with human failings. Just like Waugh and Proust, Powell was fascinated by social class, and like Waugh he had married an aristocrat and purchased a country house with the proceeds from his writing. This was The Chantry, set in a tiny Somersetshire hamlet and now lived in by John Powell, the younger of his two sons.

I'd seen one extraordinary photograph of the cloakroom and boiler room that Anthony Powell had decorated from floor to ceiling with a highly imaginative – almost surrealist – cut-out collage of newspaper and magazine scraps; John Powell very kindly invited me to visit and to lunch. His parents had bought the house from a Wing Commander Barraclough in 1952. 'It was very basic, nobody had messed around with it at all. We had paraffin heating and all that sort of thing.' His father would write successive volumes of *Dance* here: a surprise inheritance had suddenly enabled him to extend his novel sequence to 12 volumes and to decorate and improve to his heart's content. Wallpapers came from Cole & Son, except for the library's, which Powell had papered in an avant-garde asphalt-stripe by Edward Bawden. His wife, Lady Violet, made scrap screens and stitched needlework cushions there and edited his great work, chapter by chapter, each evening while he rested on the chaise longue. Powell's other *magnum opus*, his scrap-collaged mural of 'almost Sistine Chapel proportions' (as described by his nephew Ferdinand Mount), was the therapeutic pastime he turned to during bouts of insomnia or writer's block. Whenever John finds places where it is lifting away from the wall now, he gently sticks them back down.

Min Hogg

Kensington, London
2018

Min Hogg started *Interiors* magazine (as it was then called) in 1981, working from a room above a Fulham florist's shop and featuring a list of places that she 'knew from life'. I started writing for *The World of Interiors* 20 years later when she had given up being its editor, but we met here and there and shared a godson, and eventually we were friends. Min preferred houses that had been personalised by their owners and not professionally decorated, and so did I. She had collected antique textiles from the age of eight, hung her pictures edge to edge and gloried in her favourites: an Italian funeral citation above the sofa; her portrait of the seductive eighteenth-century actress Kitty Fisher; her mother's equestrian painting of Queen Victoria.

Min had met designer Nicky Haslam at a Debs dance and he became her best friend, 'by miles'. Once when he was looking for a bespoke wallpaper pattern for a client he had lent her an eighteenth-century portfolio of botanical seaweeds from which to source a design. She had got together with Michael Tighe, the former art director at *Interiors*, and 'we just couldn't stop, we went on and on, so then we found we'd got a collection'. The glorious Seaweed Collection of papers and textiles has become another legacy of this very funny, forthright, stylish, original human being.

Gretchen Andersen

Old Manor Farmhouse, Sussex

2022

It was *Interiors* magazine that sent me to interview Gretchen Andersen, long-time proprietor of The Lacquer Chest antique shop in Kensington Church Street. I had only a hazy notion of this fabled place, as my west London antiquing had always happened half a mile off in Portobello and Golborne roads. We sat down together to talk in her little terraced house, Gretchen in her favourite winged armchair, upholstered in an original William Morris wool fabric patterned with birds and flowers. 'I got it 50 years ago, nobody knew what it was,' she told me. Gretchen's conversation was addictive and far ranging, and a few months later, she and her photographer daughter, Emily Andersen, asked me to Sunday lunch at Old Manor Farmhouse, their family house in Sussex.

I called the photo story that I wrote then 'The Last of Old England' because when Gretchen and her husband, Viv, bought it in 1959, it had been condemned as 'unfit for human inhabitation'. There were brambles growing inside and three outside lavatories. The oldest end of the house dates from the fourteenth century and although there is electricity and plumbing now, it still feels as old as it looks. 'An antiques dealer in Pulborough was very supercilious, he called us Cobweb Castle,' Gretchen told me. 'A wonderful man, Mr Wells, used to live in this house with his aunt when he was a boy. And he was terribly fond of it. He used to come and paint the rooms when we were in London. Quite often, he painted the wrong room the wrong colour, because he hadn't heard properly! I was so sorry when he gave up painting.'

There are extraordinarily nice things and extraordinary things here – my favourites, the two little wooden dolls' heads carved by the brilliant, melancholic artist and poet David Jones during his time as a brother in the Guild of St Joseph and St Dominic with sculptor Eric Gill at Ditchling, standing on top of the court cupboard beneath a row of excellent cider jugs. The staircase is thriftily carpeted in kilims that didn't sell in the shop, the Delft tiles above the bathroom sink are Fablon sticky-back plastic, manufactured in the 1960s, the most brilliant piece of trompe l'oeil.

'When we were here in the summer we'd have a list of jobs to do,' Emily remembered, 'Toby and I (not so much Ben, he was too little). Polish the table, wash the windows, saw the wood! We didn't have a television set and we used to go over to the neighbour's to see *Doctor Who*.' 'Everything is such a long time ago, you just can't imagine what it was like. Oh, we had such adventures!' Gretchen said.

Manor Farm

Carlos Sánchez-Garcia

2022

Carlos Sánchez-García decorates with a keen eye. When I met him, he and his partner, Michael, were domiciled in this old brick-red Norfolk farmhouse with their three beloved dogs. They have two graceful whippets, Tristram and Theodora, but the jolliest of all is Alfred, a chihuahua–pug cross who belonged to Michael's mother, who poses enchantingly for my photographs and has a very kind face.

We are both domestic, Carlos says, we both have our own strengths. One is making jam, greengage or gooseberry, both equally delicious, and there are chickens, a big sunny garden and a barn with resident barn owl. Carlos's own taste here is for a sort of country house vernacular that's wholly appropriate for the house's age and architecture, but he makes much grander rooms for his clients. And also furniture, wallpapers and fabrics – a document wool fabric that's a lovely woven pattern from Anatolia and Kandili, a block-printed Ottoman-era linen that will become the new loose cover on my old sofa.

The word 'jolly' is a favourite of his; their kitchen is painted in Edward Bulmer's Olympian Green to jolly it up and make it more cheery. In the study, which is where Michael works, they made a new fireplace and surrounded it with Delft tiles painted by local artist Paul Bommer, who made pictures of things that meant something to them – their dogs, the church and the ruined castle at Baconsthorpe. The master bedroom, with its writing desk and four-poster, is heavenly – books, rugs, lamps, patchwork bed quilt all *comme il faut*. But I particularly liked the mushroom pink and wallpapered guest bathroom and another, half way up the stairs, with an old Jean Monro chintz; and afterwards I sent search parties into Portugal to obtain cakes of the yolk-yellow citron soap that I'd seen and smelt resting on the bath rack there. Carlos has placed potted pelargoniums everywhere, and their lemony scent percolates every room, although his Spanish mother always tells him that these plants should only be found out of doors.

WAGNER'S
'RING'
AND ITS
SYMBOLS

CLAUS
PORTO

CAMP

Wardington Manor

Bridget Elworthy
2016

I heard about the phenomenal Land Gardeners from Charlie McCormick and Ben Pentreath (see pages 71, 149 and 219). Charlie had lived with Bridget Elworthy at her country house Wardington Manor for a while, working as a woofer and then helping out with the household and Bridget's cut-flower business. Bridget and her friend Henrietta Courtauld had formed a garden design partnership and were deeply involved in trials with a magical microbial aerobic 'climate compost' that might promise a solution for all the manmade evils of modern agriculture and poor soil health. With a brilliant take on branding, they had devised their own gardening uniform of tidy navy blue smocks 'with big pockets that say the Land Gardeners on them', worn with leggings and Gertrude Jekyll-esque rubber boots, in homage to the feminist gardeners of the 1940s and 50s at the Waterperry Horticultural School for Women and their jodhpur'd principal Miss Beatrix Haversgill.

They asked me to lunch at Wardington, Charlie came back to show me around and Bridget explained about the house: her philosophy of make do-and-mend furnishing; 'just filling up rooms, really'; raids on local auction houses; and the 'emergency' vintage French bed hangings she had made and stapled up with a friend just in time for the arrival of some well-heeled guests. But they are wholly serious about what they do; the importance of soil health is what continues to preoccupy them. '*The Archers* is the best way to get the message out to farmers! We want to get hold of *The Archers*!' they cried. Their extraordinarily beautiful book, *Soil to Table* (2024), gives us the synopsis of all this and more.

Wolterton Hall

Peter Sheppard and Keith Day
2017–2021

Someone was telling me about Peter Sheppard and Keith Day one day and added 'you'd really like them'. A couple of years later I met them in a crowded room, towed across the floor like awkward water skiers by a brace of pug dogs on short leashes. I stayed with them for the first time just after they'd taken possession of Wolterton Hall in Norfolk, arriving travel-stained one Sunday at tea time to be told, 'We're giving a little dinner for you tonight!' Older friends of theirs may have grown blasé with their very considerate and generous style of hospitality, but I have not. Peter and Keith are gourmands, stylists and designers who have learned how to conjure the very best of everything in food and drink and living spaces.

Wolterton is the sister house to Houghton Hall, built at the same time by the same gang of master craftsmen for another member of the same prodigious Walpole clan, who were then in the political ascendancy in Britain. With nearly a dozen bedrooms, many of its dynastic furnishings in situ and a lake and parkland setting surpassing the landscape at Houghton, Wolterton made grand demands of them. When I first visited, it had been closed up and moribund for nearly 50 years, reroofed and redecorated in the 1950s after an attic fire, then gradually decommissioned as the family retrenched into another of their properties a few miles away. I photographed it then, and again and again during a metamorphosis in which the kitchen garden was replanted and invasive rhododendrons routed; the haha was rebuilt (sheep no longer ascended to the piano nobile and gazed in through the windows of the saloon); park railings replaced barbed wire; wool damask covered the state dining room walls; and new baths and showers gushed in marbled bathrooms where avocado and primrose-colour baths and basins had reigned.

Peter made dashing and judicious choices in auction houses and dealers' warehouses, and collaborated with Watts1874 to reproduce document wallpapers and textiles for the house. Keith did what Keith does best, spinning rooms out of the vast collection of lovely chattels that they had accumulated during successive house moves that included a stint in Bloomsbury's former Omega Workshops premises at 33 Fitzroy Square and another in a Venetian palazzo. In the photographs of Wolterton you will see superb Delft china and tiles, Venetian chairs and gondola lamps, a collection of nudes by Duncan Grant, the new 'State' lavatory and bathroom, and their extraordinary *batterie de cuisine*, precision-equipped like the deck of a sea-going battleship.

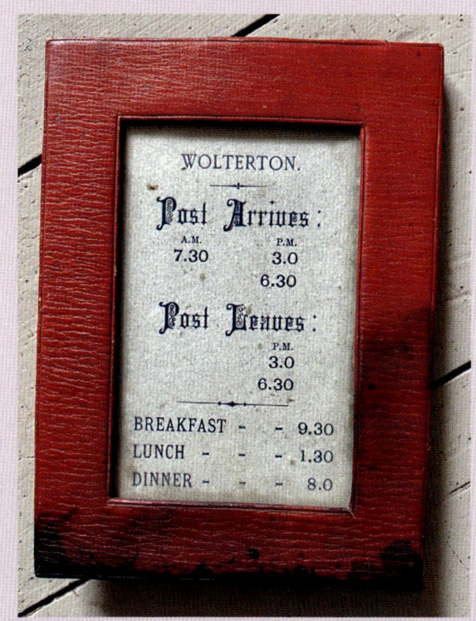
WOLTERTON.

Post Arrives:

A.M.	P.M.
7.30	3.0
	6.30

Post Leaves:

P.M.
3.0
6.30

BREAKFAST - - 9.30
LUNCH - - - 1.30
DINNER - - - 8.0

VEGETABLES
BEANS Broad
Dwarf
Runner
BEETROOT
BROCCOLI
CABBAGE
CARROTS
CAULIFLOWER
CUCUMBER
LETTUCE
MARROW
ONIONS
PEAS
RADISHES
SPINACH
SWEET CORN
TOMATOES
TURNIPS
POTATOES
PARSLEY & MINT
FRUIT
STRAWBERRIES
RASPBERRIES
CHERRIES
PEARS
APPLES
PEACHES
RHUBARB

Bettiscombe Manor

Jasper Conran
2022

While we were all locked up in our houses in the spring of 2020, I asked various friends to 'guest' for me on the bibleofbritishtaste. Jasper Conran stepped up with a beautiful sequence of photographs and a discourse about some of his dearest friends. A year or so later, on an autumnal day, I went to Dorset to take some pictures of my own.

'I promise not to tidy up', Jasper had said, 'I know you like to see toast crumbs!' – but he had only just returned from a long trip to Morocco and his housekeeper had made everything immaculate in his absence. So he thoughtfully directed me to the larder, boot room, painting studio and other possibly almost-slightly-less-than-perfect zones, and I pottered on, while he stayed in bed recuperating from his travels with a log fire lit in the grate. This is what I photographed: the vegetable garden just beginning to 'go over' (see page 232); paints and cig ends in the studio; the best ticking-striped and frilled long sofa in the sitting room; the patinated dry surfaces of ancient joinery in the scullery; and Jasper's beautiful naked foot beneath the canopy of his four-poster bed.

The Old Parsonage

Ben Pentreath and Charlie McCormick
2018–2024

This will be my last night in the Old Parsonage, in the green bedroom on the side of the house that overlooks Charlie McCormick's long herbaceous borders. Everything is utterly settled in here now: the wallpapers that Ben hung, gothic-architectural or William Morris, beginning to be scuffed; the floral hippo of a sofa that was Ben's parents' comfortably beached at the garden end of the kitchen; gardening boots under the hall table and gardening books jostling for space on tables and shelves in the sitting room. But it's lively – chickens at the back door, dogs scuttering to and fro – and the garden enfolding the house, bedding it down into cushiony foliage, the rose beds falling away down the slope to the churchyard, vegetables in schoolroom lines behind the kitchen-garden hedges.

All these accretions and siltings-up – their joyful harvestings of teacups and plates, books and pictures, animal life and super-abundant horticulture – have come about more recently, with Charlie's advent. The climax is the old flower room: half filled with his seed packets, jugs and Constance Spry vases; the other half, royal banners, patriotic bunting and shortbread tins – a museum of everything that he likes best. I wander about taking note and looking for the souvenirs – like fisherman's buoys and floats – that are the past rites and representations of our friendship: a painting of a labrador in an arbour beside Charlie's bed; the pigeon fancier's certificate that was my Collins thank you note to them both still moored to the kitchen wall just by the fridge; and their saffron-yellow wedding party invitation on the egg yolk-yellow gloss of the kitchen wall.

GOD
SAVE
THE
KING

TARIFF
BEER
Draught, per pint 7d. Glass 4d.
Bottle - - - - 5d.
Home Brewed - - 6d.
Bass, Guinness or Worthington 8d.
Cider - - - - 6d.
SPIRIT
Whisky, Gin (Special) 9d. (Soda extra)
Brandy - - 1/-
WINE
Ports, Sherry, etc.- - 8d.
MINERALS
Lemonade, Ginger Beer 4d.
Dry Ginger, Tonic Water 5d.
Sandwiches 3d. Pies 3d.
EXETER INN, HONITON
C. REAL, Proprietor
DIPLOMA OF MERIT
THIS IS TO CERTIFY

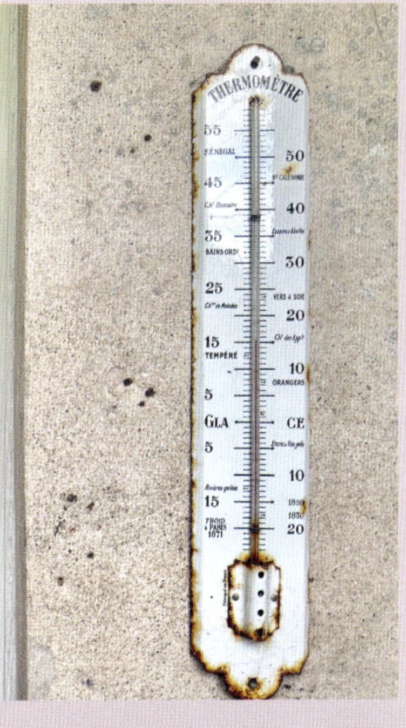
THERMOMÈTRE

VOGUE LIVING

VOGUE LIVING
GREAT HOUSES OF BRITAIN
Northumberland
Cecil Beaton AT HOME
GARDENS

Benedict Foley and Daniel Slowik

East Anglia

2021–2024

Benedict Foley and Daniel Slowik live in a house I call the Acme of Taste. It's painted pink and it stands by a confluence of lanes in a confluence of watery tributaries on the border of Essex and Suffolk. In the years I have known them, the house has evolved with them, and now – and more so than in any of the others in this book – it is 'properly' decorated. What I mean by this is that every element has been thought through and is settling down into something like a perfect whole the longer that they live here. It's a wholly different game from what I – and perhaps, you – do, which is to put things down in different places and then occasionally swap them around for a better effect; exchange a coolie lampshade for a drum, perhaps, or change the colour of the walls. Daniel cut his teeth at interior decorator's Sibyl Colefax, Benedict took inspiration from designers Geoffrey Bennison and Robert Kime. When they decorate together, their company is Nuthall Temple, named for the Palladian country house once owned by an ancestor of Daniel's.

It's a weekend place but weekends here often extend to four or five days at a stretch. There's a sandy-ochre dried-mud colour on the sitting room walls that's a perfect foil to the eau de nil-painted armoire behind the sofa that serves as their drinks cupboard, but I think this may be about to change. There are old patterns and newer fabrics that Daniel has brought into production: a drab-blue underskirt on the dining room table contrast-patterned with white ivy foliage, like a cyanotype of a chintz diaper. In the dining room, bright white paint sets off museum-quality china plates arranged by Benedict on the credenza. They are very good at finding eighteenth-century import lacquerware and orientalising furniture of a superb kind. A William IV hall chair of uncommon handsomeness is painted a rich, drab cane brown; nineteenth-century Bombay blackwood chairs from India metamorphose to bright white, the kind of transformation Syrie Maugham might have thought of but didn't.

The things I like here most are: everything about the new guest bedroom, once the shrine to an extraordinary four-poster of Cecil Beaton's, now home to neat twin divans tucked under goose-shit green blankets. That looking glass! And the red lacquer chest on a stand; and the curtains made from a very lovely and complex old patchwork quilt, extended with panels of a striped fabric. Daniel's squiggle-pattern diaper chintz, the ornamented wall brackets designed by Benedict, and his lion's paw door-stop. The garden behind the cottage, where old galvanised water tanks are stuffed with bosky planting, and the view is nothing but cows and bright green grass. Their 1950s kitchen, flood-proof, red-tiled floor, blue 'units' from decades past and gloss yellow walls. I think this house is really 'classy' – sophisticated and insouciant by turns.

THE
SUN KING
BILLY
BALDWIN
decorates

BIG

HINTLESHAM

Ashington Manor

Julian and Isabel Bannerman

2021–2024

The Bannermans came to Ashington almost half a dozen years ago, to a place stranded in time. They had found an old manor house adrift on a cement farmyard, with its gardens reduced to quickset hedges and a derelict cider orchard. The house felt a little unmoored, its domestic offices lost to a historic fire, its flat Bath-stone facades glowering orange far across the horizontal lines of the Somerset levels. But its gothic window tracery was beautiful, the outlines of its vast great hall still discernible past partitions and strange new lowered floor levels that had cut its double height in half. There was a blocky Jennifer Archer- style hand-built oak fitted kitchen jammed into one end, the fascinating survival of a brief moment of higher, more luxurious status in the 1980s, which we all rather loved. To fix this ancient place took money, patience, historic building inspectors from English Heritage, imagination, courage and perseverance, excellent artisan craftsmen and hours and hours of their time; Isabel crafting and recrafting its architectonic spaces as three-dimensional architectural models so as to understand what might best be done.

Restored at last to a state of Elizabethan grace, with a tapisserie garden (see page 214) of oranges, purples and scarlets laced with stately beehive domes of yew and mellow saffron yellow and orange plastered walls, Ashington is exquisite. Julian planted the garden and Isabel brought it indoors, finding textiles of rare beauty, a crewel bedcover embroidered by two spinster sisters, bed hangings and old glazed chintzes – some the legacy of her mother – and hanging the best guest bed with them. She dressed the sitting room sofas in blousy antique floral cottons and linens patterned with ferns, adding stripes when a pattern ran out. In high summer, all along the drive, the pointy spikes of pink orchids showed in the grass, brought back like Persephone from who knows how many years of underground dormition, beneficiaries of their great skill in husbandry.

MILTON AVERY
ANCIENT ENGLISH HOUSES
CHRISTOPHER SIMON SYKES
photographs by
YVES PARADIS

Luke Edward Hall and Duncan Campbell

Gloucestershire

2024

After years being metropolitan, Luke Edward Hall and Duncan Campbell finally rusticated in 2019. They suddenly found themselves craving the great outdoors, dogs, chintz, flowers and a garden, spare rooms for friends to stay in and somewhere to be at the weekend that wasn't an overpriced bedroom above a gastropub. They ended up in a little farmhouse with a yard in front and a meadowy back garden, rented from an estate in the Gloucestershire end of the Cotswolds, where the Chelsea tractors give way to real combine harvesters.

Duncan and Luke wanted it to feel cosy and inviting, a bit cottagey but never twee. They have mixed styles and periods with their own designs, and tried out novel experiments. The sitting room used to be painted a duck-weed green they got from Leyland, the dining room was a mustardy yellow. The former is a chalky pink now, and the dining room is a more ointment-ish raspberry colour. They've grown dahlias, mowed a twisty path through the long grass of the meadow and become the owners of one whippet, Merlin, with fur the colour of a young faun, followed by a pewter-grey one, Dragon.

Luke had a striped garden tent awning made up, fit for a tourney at Camelot, and they celebrated their wedding with a huge party here afterwards. Their Vico Magistretti green dining chairs have made the cut, along with the gold-shell grotto chair that they found in Tetbury and the pair of painted gothic chairs Luke bought from the sale of Sir Roy Strong's old Herefordshire house, The Laskett (see page 230).

Tomatoes are growing in the boot-room-cum-cloakroom now. The bedroom is a glorious muddle. A Prince of Wales tomato-soup-red investiture chair is jammed into the lavatory, which has turned from turquoise to shocking pink. The tongue-and-groove bathroom stayed a light emerald green (almost the green of Clive Bell's narrow bathroom at Charleston farmhouse that he hogged and refused to share with his household).

Luke and Duncan met when they were both about 19 years old. Together and separately they have achieved a perfect alchemy – in colourways, stuff, florals, dressing up and down, food and drink and ways of living. In the 'drinks tray' alcove there's a gun-metal owl that I completely love and covet, modelled as a perfect silvery ice bucket.

HOWARD

BABY
JET
OUTSIDE IN
DAVID HOCKNEY BY
HERBERT LIST

David Hicks
home decor

BITTER LEMON
WELCH

CHATEAU ORLANDO
Austin Austin
Austin Austin

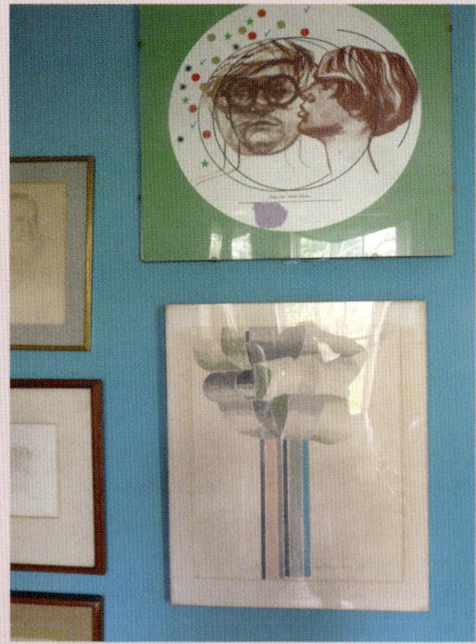

WE SHALL FIGHT
WE WILL WIN
PARIS
LONDON
DEMAND
ALL POWER TO THE CAMPUS SOVIETS!
I SHALL VOTE LABOUR

Hilaire Gomer

Southwark, London

2013

A large family grew up in this Thames-side villa, cunningly decorated by their mother, Hilaire Gomer, whose own very stylish mother 'Ba' Eustace had kept an antiques shop at the more amusing end of Chelsea's King's Road. These are well-lived-in rooms where the surpluses and excesses are crammed onto shelves or kicked under the sofas. In the ground-floor double drawing room, walls are a vivid deep turquoise on the garden side, and a strong jade green in the room at the front. I doubt that Farrow & Ball does any shades half so nice.

Hilaire is a colourist and says that her dear mother decorated like this in the 1960s, largely using the new paint range by Terence Conran. This is her philosophy:

I have had a thing about peacock colours for quite a while and let rip in green and turquoise in the double drawing room, courtesy of good old Dulux. The colours are rather alarming and would put off most sane people, but they are dampened down by many pictures which always thrive on block colour. I would always counsel colour for a decorating statement, especially if the decorator doesn't own many pictures or much clutter. You have to have something for the eye to latch on to.

The downstairs lavatory is painted inferno red, displaying the anarchist tracts and furious manifestoes of the late poet Christopher Logue, contributed by Hilaire's husband.

Jane MacEwan

Badminton Estate, Gloucestershire
2023

Jane MacEwan is a painter and landscape gardener (see page 213) who divides her time between her cottage in Wales and the old schoolhouse she shares with Gerald Harford on the Badminton Estate. Thirty years ago the duke's estate carpenters made it into a habitable space for them, with an upper floor and beautiful flying staircase that runs around the huge double-height hall. *Macleaya cordata* in a green jug stands on a green leather-topped oval Georgian table made for the Bristol bank founded by Gerald's ancestors.

Behind a door to the right is Jane's studio, piled with stacks of antique picture frames and her works in progress. The drawing room under the tall pitched roof of the old schoolroom is extraordinary, its long windows hung with antique crimson damask curtains repurposed from a Majorcan castle. Jane mixed the putty green distemper for the walls and limed the old floorboards below to a silvery grey. Gerald's three-time great grandfather hangs over the mantle, Admiral Nelson's favourite midshipman Sir William Hoste. All their shared belongings are settled and silted down together in this cool, graceful house.

BRIDGE TO REMBRANDT
PAOLO UCCELLO
PATINIR
Bosch
PINTORICCHIO AT SPELLO
Van Gogh
HOWARD HODGKIN
IN A NEW LIG
PONTORMO
Vermeer and the Delft School

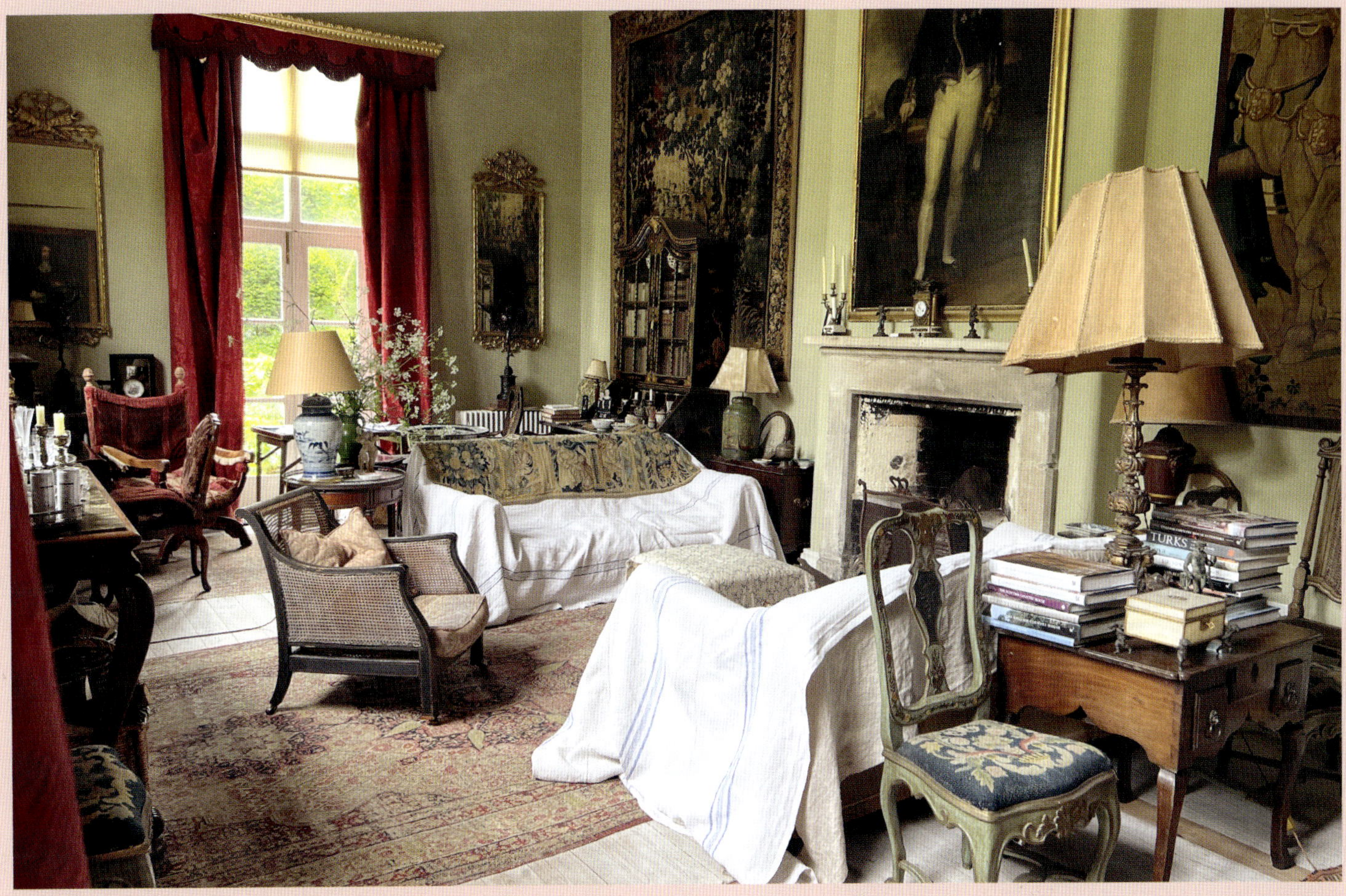
TURKS

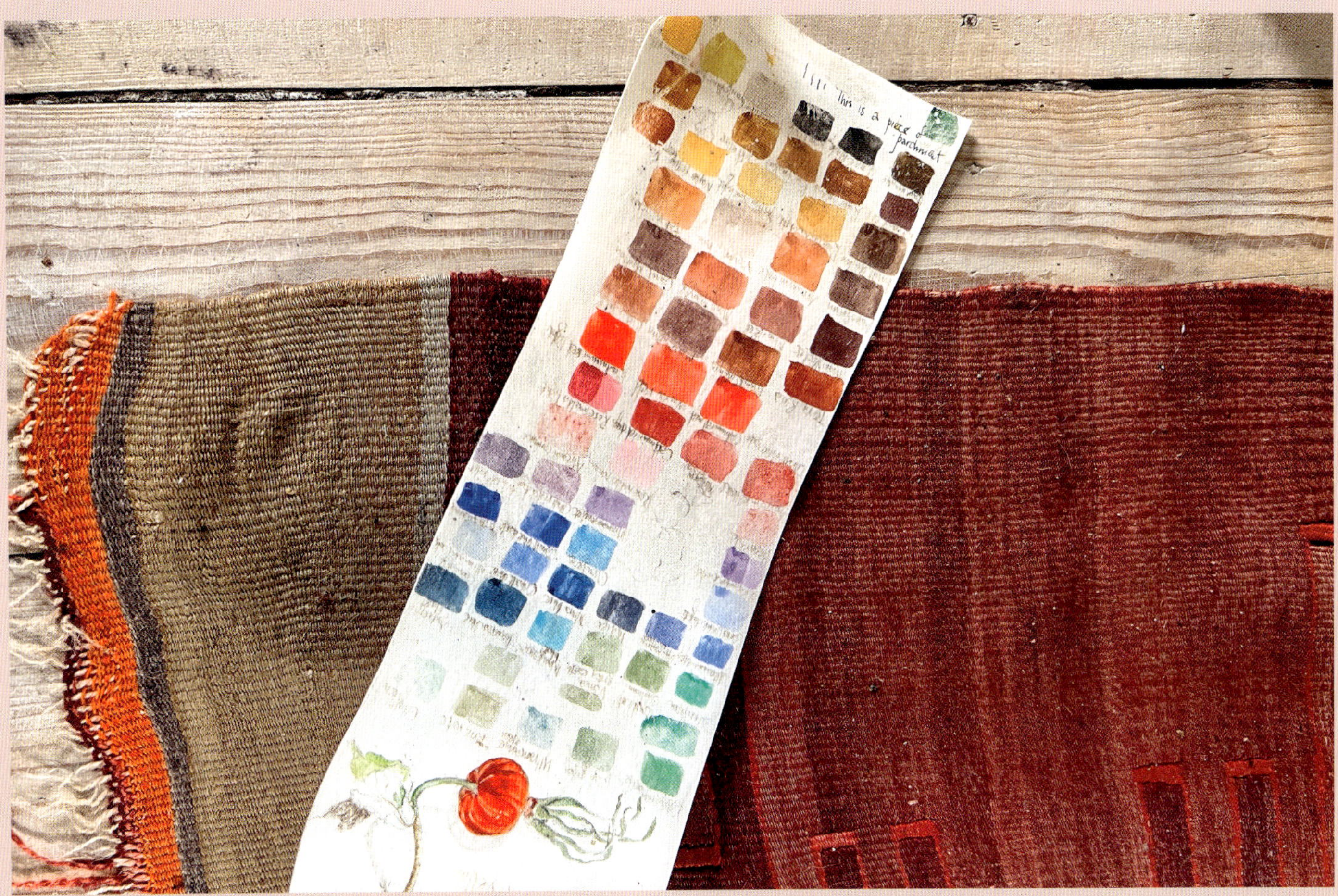
This is a piece of
parchmat

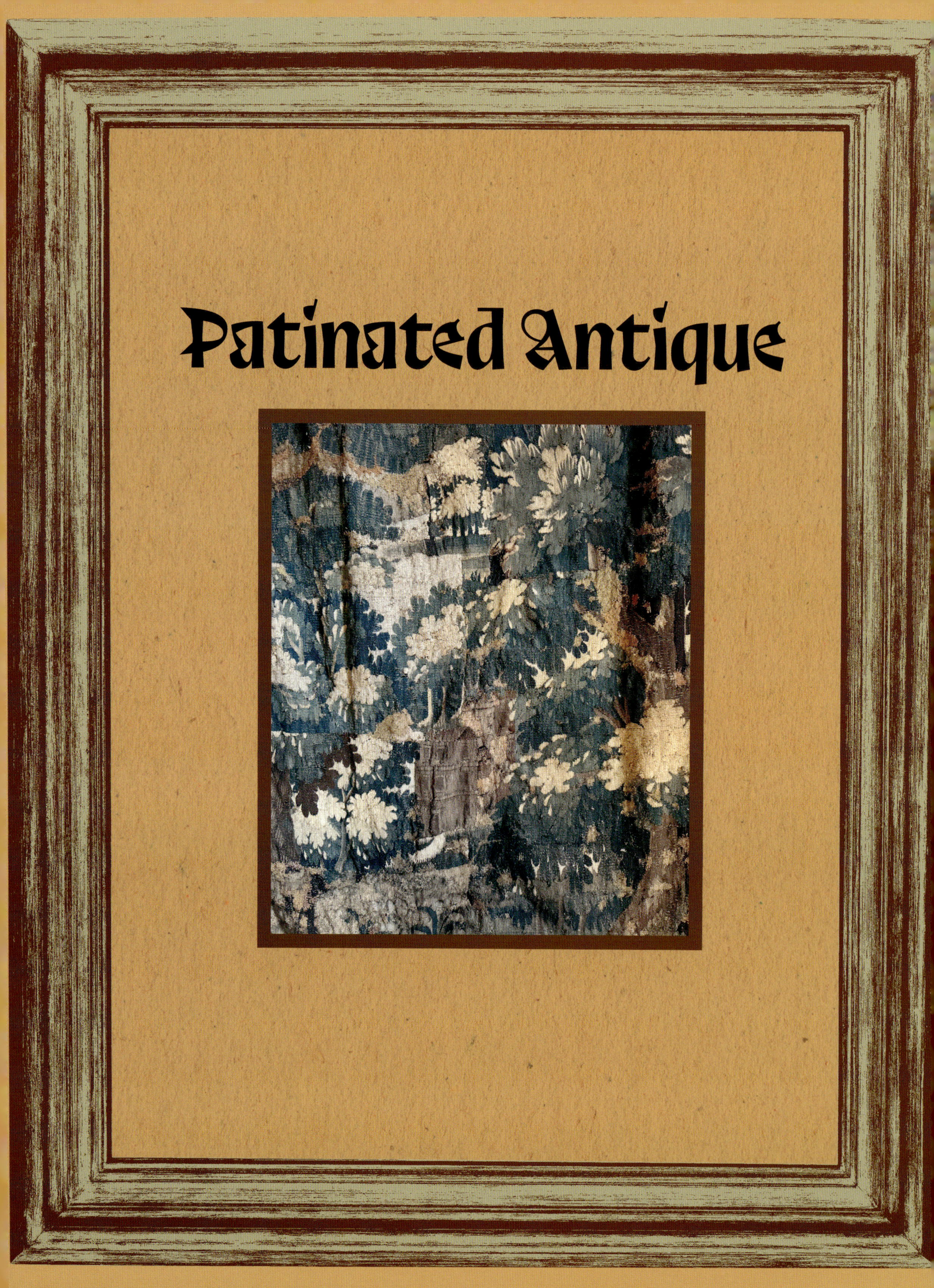
Patinated Antique

I telephoned my friend Ben Pentreath and asked him to help me solve a riddle: Why do we all want our houses to look old and full of old stuff? Is there an element of snobbery, a quest for 'authenticity,' 'romance', a false hindsight that holds the past as a much better place? We talked for half an hour without reaching any very exact conclusions. Ben said that so many people's homes nowadays looked as if they had been decorated by AI – the similar light fittings, kitchens, sofas, colours, all sourced from global giants like Ikea and filtered through the prism of Instagram and Pinterest. A new trend, design twist or colour arrives, the early adopters and style gurus stake their claims and broadcast their photographs, a single image swirls through the algorithms, from Helsinki to Tokyo to Madrid, and is immediately everywhere; a decade of Instagram has condensed and accelerated this trend.

Once, 20 years ago and after long deliberation, I chose a bedroom wallpaper from the venerable company Cole & Son (founded in 1875), a sweet Victorian trellis that seemed irresistibly and uniquely of its time. Then a couple of years later I began to see it here and there again and again, in magazines, glimpsed through a lit-up window, recommended by a decorator and finally, on a hot, smoggy day in Jaipur, prettily trellising the walls of a tiny 'English' café where we drank some tea. I had dipped a toe in the water at the onset of a taste tidal wave sweeping the Western and Eastern continents and as globally ubiquitous as Coca-Cola, and I wasn't at all pleased.

So the houses that follow are an antidote to this kind of mass-culture modernity, for they are some of the most deeply patinated dwellings I know, houses built of old bricks, with silted-up attics and palimpsests of decorative finishes layered upon walls that are close and carelessly picture-hung and speaking of long human occupancy. Shulbrede Priory, the very oldest and perhaps the most extraordinary of all, owes its metamorphosis from religious house to country house to the romantic tenets, pieties and preservationist practices of the Arts and Crafts movement. The gentle translation that took it from its ruinous state did not disturb or rout the bats that roost in the rafters of its high Great Chamber or its furry mantles of lichen; there have been no zany schemes of redecoration or new plumbing. Ancient Beckley and Wolfeton and Charlecote have had nothing of the modern imposed upon them, lived in 'as found' by owners who behave as the guardians and custodians of these places. And Smedmore House has passed down from family member to family member, by marriage and by descent, for 700 years.

Beckley Park

Amanda Feilding

2024

Down a long farm track not far from the dreaming spires of Oxford but very far from the madding crowd, is Beckley Park. It was built in the 1540s of small, mauve-red Tudor bricks, a three-towered hunting lodge islanded by three medieval moats near the wetlands of Otmoor. As soon as I got out of my car in the stable yard I was joined by a little heraldic white dog who gave me a quick friendly look, then set off, glancing back at me to follow. It led me to the front door, through topiary and over a medieval bridge and moat, and when I pulled a jangling bell it trotted busily away.

The unicorn-like magical dog belongs to Amanda Feilding, aka Lady Amanda Neidpath, Countess of Wemyss and March. It matches the spirit of this place, a 'Grand Meaulnes', Lost Domain spirit, for Beckley has survived unaltered for 500 years, during which it was owned by the Earls of Abingdon and latterly tenanted by farmers. Amanda's grandmother Clothilde found and bought it in 1920, 'for the romance of the place'. She and her husband, Percy, had trained with the architect and landscape designer Reginald Blomfield and could see how best to work with what was here. Percy devised an extraordinary pyramidal topiary garden, thickets of pointed geometry crammed between the back of the house and the innermost moat.

Amanda grew up rather solitary here, companioned by pets and imaginary friends, discovering mystical worlds: 'I had plenty of time to mooch around dreaming. Then in 1965, aged 16, she got into psychedelics and concluded that this was fertile ground. All her energies and resources have been channelled into research on the unfathomed potential offered by psychedelics ever since. Amanda founded the Beckley Institute, treading a lonely path that is only now being adopted and endorsed by the medical and scientific establishments and big pharma. *The Daily Mail* keeps a keen eye on all her doings, dubbing her 'Lady Mindbender', a name she's quite enjoyed owning.

When her parents died, she came back to live at Beckley, raising the funds to buy out her siblings. Her Beckley is very little changed. 'Let's go up to my old room,' she says, climbing the twisting wooden spiral.

From its projecting bay in the top of a tower, three diamond-leaded Elizabethan windows look out over fat wodges of sculpted topiary, water beyond and deer park. Sepia-bleached tapestries and tattered velvet curtains like martial banners line and frame the spine corridor and its doorways down the length of the house.

Amanda has predicted that psychedelics can offer healing for depression, trauma, addiction, autism, mental illness, age-related and neuro-degenerative conditions and better outcomes for palliative care. Used properly, psychedelics will help mankind to live and to think better. Magical Beckley, with its deep roots into the past, is where all this begins. 'I think of it as part of my soul,' she says.

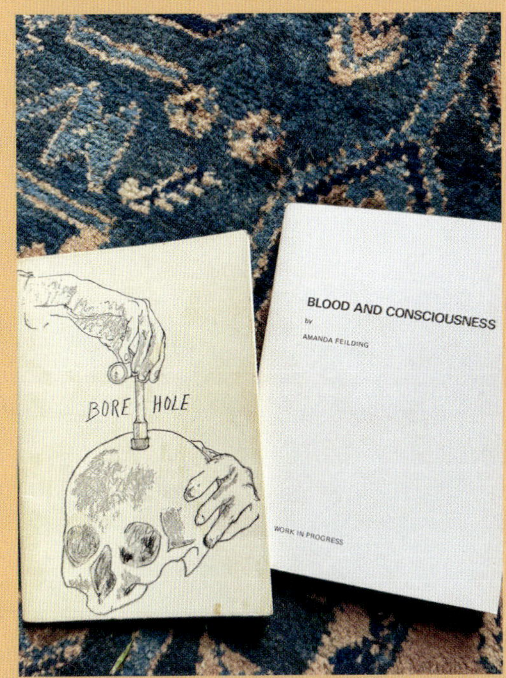
BORE HOLE
BLOOD AND CONSCIOUSNESS
by
AMANDA FEILDING
WORK IN PROGRESS

Shulbrede Priory

Catherine Ponsonby and Ian Russell
2016–2024

Sir Hubert Parry was a Victorian composer of incandescent melodies. He set the words of William Blake's 'Jerusalem' to its lusty tune and composed the electrifying anthem 'I was glad when they said unto me' that is sung at every coronation. In the 1920s Parry's daughter Dorothea and her new husband Arthur Ponsonby set up home at Shulbrede Priory, a tumbledown farmhouse built into the ruined medieval walls of a religious house suppressed under Henry VIII's reformist zeal.

They were high-minded souls, intellectuals and Fabians tuned into the zeitgeist for Arts and Crafts and the slumbering relics of olden times, so theirs was a conservative approach to home making. They added on a low-ceiled wing, water closets and the occasional bathroom, but adopted the Prior's high chamber, with its ancient wall paintings, for a drawing room, and made their dining room in the remaining part of the medieval refectory below. For furnishings they favoured tapestry, oak, Morris chintzes and rush-seated chairs. Arthur sat in the freezing undercroft cellar writing an antiquarian history of his new house.

Their decorating style might be described as 'intellectual socialist', but their daughter Elizabeth Ponsonby rebelled, becoming one of the leaders of the Bright Young Things and, supposedly, the model for Evelyn Waugh's poignant character Agatha Runcible. Waugh described the BYT's pastimes as 'Masked parties, Savage parties, Victorian parties, Greek parties, Wild West parties, Russian parties, Circus parties, parties where one had to dress as somebody else, almost naked parties in St John's Wood'. Since the 1970s, Ian Russell, his wife Catherine, (granddaughter of Arthur and Dorothea), their children and now their grandchildren have been here, changing very little. They keep Elizabeth's old doll's house in the dining room, for it's a 'working doll's house', always ready for action.

The ancient stones and fabric of Shulbrede teem with living things. Catherine's sister Laura Ponsonby was an expert botanist who lectured on fungi, liverworts and lichens, and once helped the police in a case of murder by poisoning, identifying some deadly nightshade baked in a pie. She used to say that there were enough different species colonising the furry garden bench that stands opposite the front door to teach a complete course of mosses and liverworts. Rare long-eared bats – a species protected by law – have always roosted in the rafters of the high chamber, and their droppings have pitted a pointillist stipple pattern onto every piece of old wooden furniture below.

GINGER BEER

Wolfeton House

Captain Nigel and Katherine Thimbleby

2010–2021

Years ago I spent a couple of weeks chauffeuring a distinguished architectural historian around the country houses that were the subject of his last big book. We went to houses so remote and carefully private that I had never found them in any reference book, but my favourite of all was in Dorset, at the end of a carriage drive shattered by potholes where lazy sheep dung and doze upon the warm stones. Captain Nigel Thimbleby and his wife, Katherine (nee Weld, of Lulworth Castle), lived here, at Wolfeton, hidden in plain sight right next to Dorchester. Nigel loved this house that his clever mother and he had bought together in the 1950s, loved talking about it and showing it off. A few years ago I went back there, invited by them to campaign against the developers threatening their demesne and in support of the tranquil status quo.

Wolfeton was a substantial medieval house that was enlarged and improved in the sixteenth century, and then very much left alone until parts were demolished in the 1820s. The Thimblebys had found it dilapidated and subdivided into flats. Nigel's regiment was the 11th Hussars, 'Those were the happiest days to be a soldier, because we didn't have many enemies and those we did have didn't have anything to shoot at us with.' Invalided out of the army, he joined Christie's auction house as their regional representative. 'My hunting ground was south Hampshire. I was quite interested in furniture. I never made a major mistake, put it that way. I absolutely loved it because I had to look at everything from tribal art to Picasso – well that is tribal art, isn't it?'

Wolfeton's Elizabethan carvings and plasterwork are extraordinary, figured with unicorns, Native Americans, Roman soldiers and fantastical grotesqueries. The Thimblebys demolished five pokey rooms-worth of nineteenth-century partitions to give the Long Gallery back its sense and shape, and they replaced some of its dangerously rotten floorboards. A previous owner had simply laid old copies of *Country Life* over the worst places and instructed visitors 'NOT TO STEP on the magazines'. There are no ceiling lights or modern heating in the main reception rooms, just the odd table lamp and mid-twentieth-century electric fires with long snaking flexes, but 'It's an agreeable house to live in,' Nigel said. I asked to photograph Captain Thimbleby's study with its reefs of paper and books obliterating the desk made for Admiral Hardy, who had served with Nelson at Trafalgar. 'It's going to be a horrid photograph,' he remarked, stoically.

DORSET
1900–1999
The Twentieth Century in Photographs
DAVID BURNETT
Henry Cecil
HOOF-BEATS
THROUGH MY HEART
A life shared with horses
DAVID EDELSTEN

High Hall

Alan Dodd

2013

By contrast, Alan Dodd's seventeenth-century folly, locally known as 'Mustard-pot Hall' because of its shape, is small. Dodd, a painter and muralist, lives part-time in London's sooty Caledonian Road but he loves and tends to this little Suffolk house much more assiduously. He has spent years restoring its plasterwork and internal fabric after a fire damaged its upper chamber and staircase, and he has added a set of salvaged chinoiserie-latticed windows to enhance the flat-roof 1960s extension housing the kitchen. His kitchen is full up *à la* Elizabeth David, for he is a very good cook. Greed is a factor, he says.

Dodd is an inveterate collector of good china, pretty taxidermy – long before it came back into vogue – and pictures. There's a four-poster guest bed that he designed to frame an antique needlework-panelled headboard and the Regency-striped tented library–bedroom in which he sleeps. The walls of the spine corridor are hung with a printed crimson gothic linen designed by George Gilbert Scott for the Houses of Parliament and ceiled by Dodd with 'romantic interior style' oak-grained latticework *à la* Abbotsford. There are no 'comfy' chairs. For as long as I have known him, he has been saving up to rebuild its tall, fire-damaged chimney with the salvaged handmade bricks stacked under a tarpaulin against the kitchen wall, and one day, when his ship comes in, he surely will.

Charlecote Park

Sir Edmund and Erica Fairfax-Lucy
2024

The clocks stopped in 1946, when the National Trust took possession of Charlecote's great rooms. When last I visited, the rooms were jumbled with step ladders and plastic sheeting for performative 'housekeeping', the mid-week visitors uncertain whether they were getting their money's worth. Behind a jib door is another, Narnia world, the family wing that's been home to Sir Edmund and Erica Fairfax-Lucy and their sons. Ed (as he preferred to be called) was reluctant to take up his inheritance at first, arriving in the 1960s to camp out with friends from the Royal Academy Schools in Charlecote's freezing, abandoned rooms. But he enjoyed the rooms' theatrical feeling of abandoned stage-set, with every cupboard opening on the clothes of long-dead inhabitants, their trinkets, pocket-books and spectacles. In the miraculously intact bedrooms last decorated in the nineteenth century, carpets are worn back to whipcord, damasks are shattered by sunlight and wallpapers mottle. The nursery with its three iron beds is freighted with ancestral toys and leftovers – a fort, a rocking horse, fanged taxidermy and midget lace-up boots. But when they came to live here in the 1990s, there was no domestic set-up and 'nothing much to sit on, really,' Erica says.

The living rooms came about gradually, Ed inventing their settled-looking kitchen from a service passage, laying diamond-pattern flagstones and mixing and applying colour onto plaster walls and furniture, scumbled greys on the kitchen cupboard and magenta red for the sink counter, then hanging long dropping curtains gridded with a blue and red pattern of his own devising. Everything was carefully thought out in accordance with his convictions, notions and principles. The little gun room off the kitchen became a dining room and treasure house, crammed with china, Venetian glass and *nature morte* assemblages of shells and curiosities. The geometry of Ed's formal topiary laid out in front of the Elizabethan gatehouse seems modern, but its proportions are calculated to echo the Renaissance architectural formulae he learned from studying perspective.

But painting was his vocation, and so this house became his subject. He painted throughout Charlecote's rooms and on the terrace looking out across the park, a solitary pursuit driven by a kind of philosophical enquiry. There were many interiors, unpeopled, inspired by Dutch Old Masters. He once said that he painted the space between objects, light, time, memory or something of which he was not quite sure. Erica remembers him each time she turns on the light, for she and their sons, Patrick and Johnny, often cooked supper in the almost-dark so that he could catch the last gleams of daylight, and cramped themselves into one corner of the kitchen table while his still-life spread out over the rest of it. His last painting stands on its easel at one corner of the kitchen table, just where he was painting it.

Ellis Peters

Trereife House

Tim and Elizabeth Le Grice
2018–2022

Trereife was a distinguished-looking old house I could see from the back road between Penzance and Newlyn, settled on the top slope of a gentle green paddock. I knew that it belonged to Tim and Elizabeth Le Grice, having seen them on the television programme *Country House Rescue*, watching gleefully as Tim trounced its high-handed presenter Ruth Watson by politely ignoring all her strenuous advice. I wrote a letter, tentatively asking if I might see the house, and Tim invited me for an interview. He and Liz were cautious but welcoming. I was enchanted by the way they lived here: Liz's pleasure in paintings and pottery she had collected and the anecdotes of her career as the county's art librarian; Tim's two bloodstock mares and his past as a gentleman jockey; their shared humour and *laissez faire*. They have become friends, and I have never tired of visiting Trereife, now with their daughter Georgina and her husband Will Chapman as its new chatelaines. It's an Elizabethan house that was rebuilt in Queen Anne style in the early eighteenth century by John Nicholls, whose family crest – painted on the hall chairs – is a British saddleback hog passant. A century later, young Charles Valentine Le Grice arrived to tutor widowed Mary Nicholls's young son, married her and outlived them both to become the scion of this house.

Nearly all the furnishings are inherited, but a stout seventeenth-century court cupboard in the dining room was donated by a local man who had been left it by his Welsh granny. Tim's study in the old kitchen was piled with paper and equestrian magazines, pictures of the Grand National hung above his desk.

During Tim's childhood all their furniture was put into the attic and Trereife was let to a Miss Cherry and Miss Chapman, who ran it as a failing old people's home and omitted to pay the rent. One day Tim and a friend were bicycling on the drive 'and a lorry came down, they were doing a runner, leaving the house dirty, rat-infested and painted in strange colours'. Tim's father and mother, Charles and Wilmay, moved back in, and Charles experimented with flower farming, growing violets, anemones and early daffodils that were packed in the flower loft about the stables and sent up to market on the London train. But when Wilmay tried to join in she was told, 'Mrs Le Grice, you are not Cornish, you will never learn how to make a pasty and you will never learn how to manage violets, and we're not going to tell 'ee.' The Cornish did not really like people 'from away', she had to conclude.

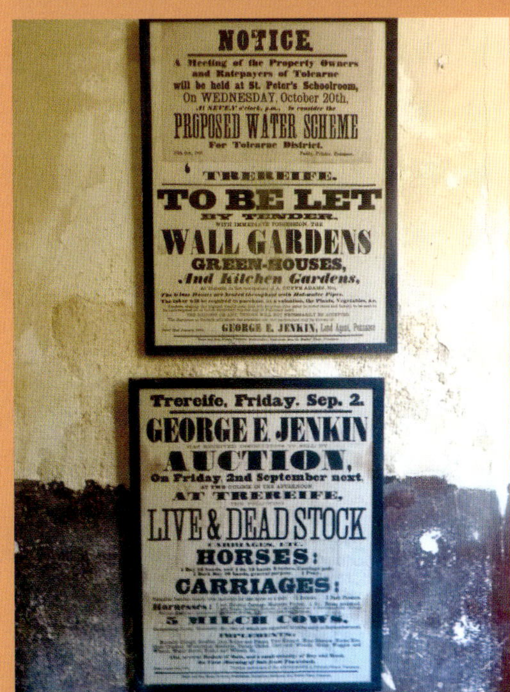
NOTICE
A Meeting of the Property Owners
and Ratepayers of Tolcarne
will be held at St. Peter's Schoolroom,
On WEDNESDAY, October 20th,
AT SEVEN o'clock, p.m., to consider the
PROPOSED WATER SCHEME
For Tolcarne District.
TREREIFE.
TO BE LET
BY TENDER.
WITH IMMEDIATE POSSESSION, THE
WALL GARDENS
GREEN-HOUSES,
And Kitchen Gardens,
GEORGE E. JENKIN, Land Agent, Penzance
Trereife, Friday. Sep. 2.
GEORGE E. JENKIN
AUCTION,
On Friday, 2nd September next,
AT TREREIFE,
LIVE & DEAD STOCK
HORSES:
CARRIAGES:
Harnesses:
5 MILCH COWS.
IMPLEMENTS:

Restoration House

Jonathan Wilmot and Robert Tucker

2021

In 1992 Jonathan Wilmot and Robert Tucker bought an old house with 120 windows that had been falling down for 300 years. Restoration House in Rochester had had one saviour before and it had broken him. The comedian and emu ventriloquist Rod Hull had bought it in 1978, tried to restore the Grade I listed house and bankrupted himself in the process, leaving outstanding repairs costed at 2 million pounds. Robert already knew how to use and mix distemper and limewash and oil linseed paint, and thought they could take it on.

Robert now spends all his time directing operations here, sleuthing, scraping old paint, mending and buying (and selling) wonderful things, then welcoming visitors in summer. The charming Gainsborough overdoor panel was sold to the pair as two very dirty landscape sketches with a weak attribution, then their picture restorer told them, 'Do you realise, they are one painting?'

There were so many things I coveted, but I liked the morning room, their two bedrooms and the barely improved bathrooms the most. The morning room has triste, mottled mica wallpaper in a Regency block-print design and a collection of black japanned lacquer ware and chinoiserie, and little, dark portraits that suit its quietist mood. In Richard's bedroom everything is very precise: his drawing board, gingham bedspread and the lustrous paintings hanging inside every square of its panelling; the bathroom with its raw brick and broken joinery has a kind of archaeology-architecture. Jonathan's bedroom trumps everything for beauty, with a verdure tapestry behind the headboard, wide waxed elm floorboards and another Gainsborough landscape bought as a 'sleeper'. Everywhere there is old paint and trompe l'oeil strapwork decoration revealed by painstaking dry-scraping.

Best of all they practise a liberal opening regime with an excellent teashop and access to the long, verdant garden. 'I think the house has become Robert's work of art,' says Jonathan. There's a consistency and a kind of quality of insight that arises over many years now – that's what you see.'

Malplaquet House

Todd Longstaffe-Gowan and Tim Knox
2016

I met Todd Longstaffe-Gowan and Tim Knox at a friend's dinner table when we were all quite young. They asked me back to their place for suppers of pasta and Berry Brothers Good Ordinary Claret, 10 of us crammed into their north London mansion flat with antique taxidermy and cathedral-sized religious art. It was more fun than I'd had for ages, so one Saturday I let them lead me to their favourite Portobello taxidermy dealer to buy a badger-like stuffed dog, costing more money than I could quite afford. I hoped I had joined their club then, although I've bought nothing of consequence since, while their ever-growing house museum in Stepney Road became justly famous, and so did they.

When Tim and Todd retreated to a much larger country house with a huge rambling garden, I was granted a final visit to Stepney and Malplaquet House. Fifteen years earlier they had celebrated its purchase with a kind of demolition party in the cavernous downstairs space that housed a defunct business fitting car exhaust pipes, their guests holding plastic cups of red wine and kicking carbon-blackened chrome tubes across the cement floor. Then the Spitalfields Trust began piecing back the house's seventeenth-century interiors, uncovering panelling, Delft tiles and shattered woodwork from among the debris and carting out 200 cubic yards of rubble. Tim and Todd completed the job with antique ironmongery and an extreme non-fitted kitchen built from scrap, leaving old brittle hair plaster and dry woodwork undecorated. Tim is a museum director who is now running the Royal Collection Trust; Todd is a garden designer, plantsman and author of high repute. The house museum he and Tim made here became famous for its sheer visual extraordinariness. Just as the first crates were being packed, I wandered through the still-crowded rooms with my camera. The sun shone in through dusty windows and motes of dust shimmered in slotted bars of bleaching light.

TO ROOF
ONLY

toppstiles

Smedmore House

Dr Philip Mansel

2014–2024

Here is Smedmore House, in its green declivity between ridge-backed Purbeck Hills. The oldest back parts of the house date only from the 1600s, but the de Smedemores were living in a house on these lands three centuries before this. The estate has never been sold, passing down and down by inheritance through the centuries. Now it belongs to Dr Philip Mansel, a scholar, historian and Francophile who is the most diverting, sophisticated person I know. Smedmore lies above the fossil-rich stony-backed beach at Kimmeridge in a green zone that has been leased by the Lulworth army training ranges and tank gunnery school since around the time of the First World War, when the British invented the tank. The pounding guns keep other kinds of human interference at bay; creating a haven for hares and owls, cuckoo flowers and cow parsley – and you go back a hundred years in time.

Downstairs there are grand eighteenth-century-looking rooms, with superb plasterwork by the Bastard brothers of Blandford Forum; upstairs the wide floorboards and blocky cornices belong to the 1600s. When Philip inherited in 1989, his friend the tastemaker Gervase Jackson-Stops helped him to redecorate. Gervase was a super-aesthete, guardian of the National Trust's historic houses, a vivid character with a whim of iron and a stammer that ran out of control in times of high emotion or when encountering the 'wrong' kind of taste. It was he who chose and mixed the dining room's perfect Tintoretto-pink walls, graduating the colour to become lighter as it rises upwards.

Philip and his partner Zeki are the curator-creators of a little family museum and a Turkish room beyond the panelled sitting room that was once Smedmore's entrance hall, enticements for the open days when the curious public come in. I think that as time passes, Philip is growing into his house like a tree growing against a wall. He and Zeki are buying it carefully selected presents: Delft and Persian vases and Ottoman carpets in rich ochre pinks and blues to ornament its empty spaces; a set of 'Schoolroom' prints for the kitchen walls. His ancestors have tended to hang on to things – a chair made for the Emperor Napoleon in the hall, drawers and vitrines full of dynastic pince-nez, snuff and trinket boxes, locks of dead hair, pocket-books and ribbon-tied bundled letters written in sepia.

There's one little apricot-washed bedroom at the back with the most fantastical rococo fireplace, worthy of a Fragonard. In the garden under a tree where you would expect to find long dead dogs' graves, there's the mossy tombstone of a tiger – so it's said? Behind the stable block, long grass and fields spread out and away and a small boat lies beached among nettles. As night falls, hunting owls cry us to sleep.

AMSTEL V. MINDEN
SINDICO
HEEMSKERKE
NYEUWENVELDE
T NYEVELT ZUYLEN
ZUYLEN DE VECHT

Steple
Vit Owre
Bridges and Howard
Owre
Viche
New Mills
PVRBEK
Alter Mills
Corfe
Aylywood
Wulgerston

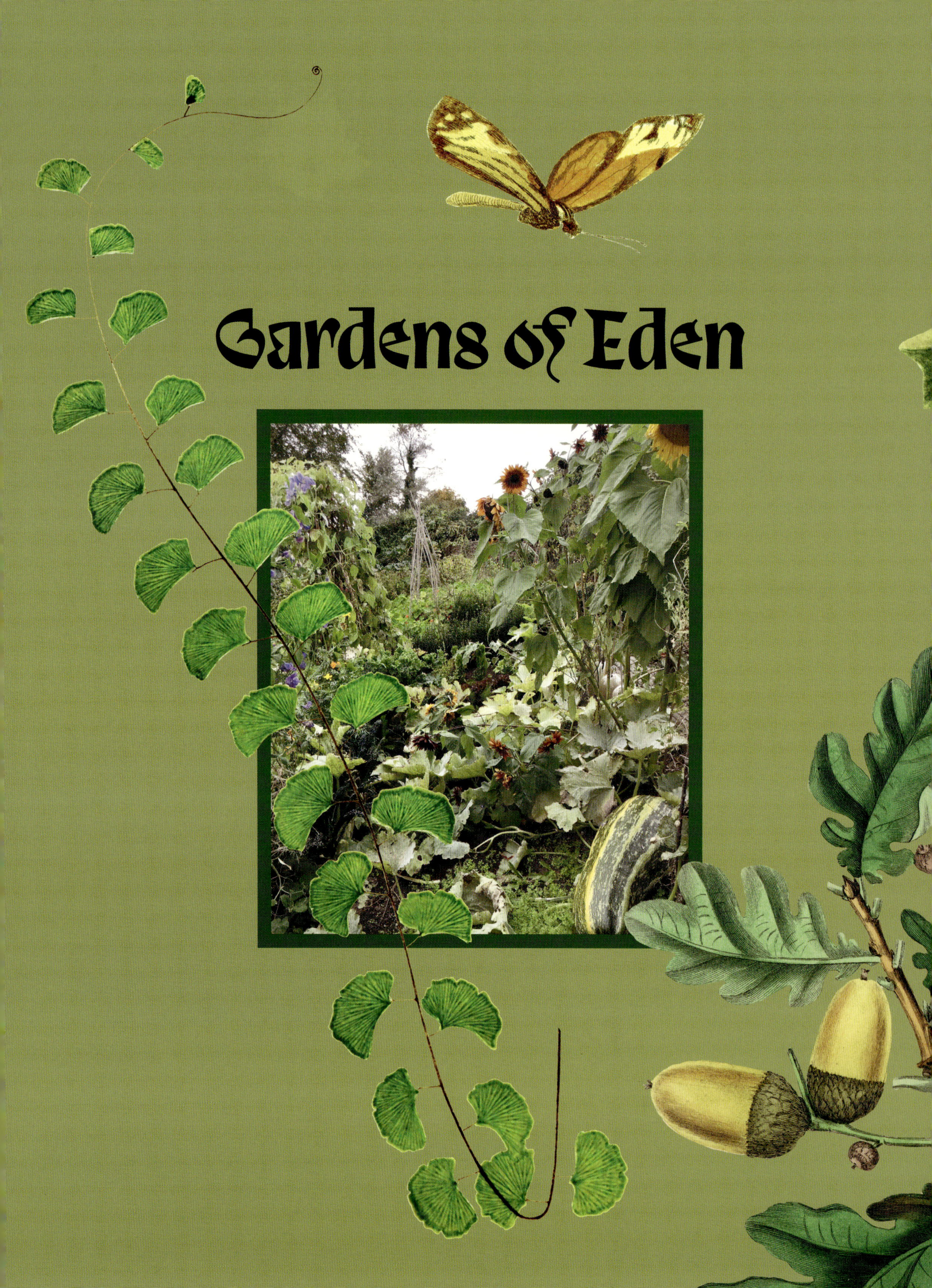

Gardens of Eden

I've just moved house again, the seventh, or possibly, eighth, house move in my grown-up life. The benison with this new house to the north of Kentish Town is a long narrow garden with walls of old stock brick, our house being slightly older than the Victorian terraces around it, standing on what were once the 'greens' or pastures where cows and their dairy maids supplied north London's fresh milk. We don't aim to move again so gardening is all the rage. But much of this garden lies under a carapace of poured concrete and crazy paving, which lifted to reveal clay sub-soil thickened with rubble and gnarly root. Next door there's a high, matted tree canopy of bay, holly and an ancient yew long ago tended and topiarised by the writer Jeanette Winterson, but now thrusting shaggily upwards and outwards. So while we seed and plant and water my expectations stay low, for this I know – that my friends all have better gardens than me.

Jane MacEwan

Badminton Estate, Gloucestershire

2023

The stakes are high. Jane MacEwan (who I first met by great good luck at a funeral wake) made her garden on the derelict plot behind her old schoolhouse, which stands just a couple of dozen steps from the gates of Badminton Park. Nothing was growing there but one venerable apple tree. On a cool day in early May last year, the 'lawn' was calf-high, surging and foaming with drenched wild grasses and cow parsley that met and marched with the borders, full up with guelder rose, starry little cranesbill flowers and spattered with blossom. There's yew here too, but in fat corkscrew spirals and swooping walled hedges, cut infrequently so that, in keeping with the nature of this place, there are no clean clipped outlines but rather blurry blocks of green upon more green.

Jane nursed the wild flowers and Queen Anne's lace into this verdure tapestry of her own making, and while I was there she dug out roots and collected seeds for me to take away. A perfectionist, she is simultaneously proud of what she has created and thoroughly discontented. I know that she's been 30 years' labouring in the making of this garden, that all of its ragged, ruffled natural wilderness is here by her art craft and toil. This is not nature tamed but rather crossbred and coaxed, coming into a relaxed flourishing, a life's work.

Ashington Manor

Julian and Isabel Bannerman

2020–2024

Adam and Eve were the first gardeners, but the Bannermans make a new Eden wherever they find themselves. I found them first at Hanham Court, near Bath, for they always seem to gravitate westwards, though often speaking recklessly of the flatlands of East Anglia. Hanham's gardens had achieved a kind of completion, with their signature green oak obelisks and yew topiary, a long terrace jettying out into space, a meadow at the foot of a scarp slope, and the elderly sheep that Isabel had got from our friend Candida Lycett Green to walk about on it and look picturesque from the house's windows. A few years later they were off, to the daring experiment of a lease from the Duchy of Cornwall at Trematon Castle, its ancient keep, embattled gatehouse and the regency villa enclosed within, looking across Plymouth Sound, the waters it was built to guard. Here, in a frenzy of creation, amazing feats were wrested from the nothingness of an abandoned double-walled kitchen garden thicketed with ash saplings, sycamore and bramble, native flora smothered under winter heliotrope, castle walls mortared with damp mosses, lichens and rare ferns. Inside these walls that were sheltered, warm and wet they worked with nature towards a pre-Raphaelite mood, coaxing back a tapisserie carpet of wild flowers, banking up the walls with spires of foxgloves and delphiniums, creating a bath of scents and smells.

And then off again, to the Somerset levels and the surviving chunk of a romantic tawny-stone Elizabethan house stranded on the cement apron of a defunct dairy farm. Through winter floods and Covid, and a complicated feat of precision engineering, the Bannermans reknitted the fabric of the house, supplied its defects and made a new garden that seems always to have been there. A first, temporary Covid garden was bedded out *faute de mieux* with anything they could buy in local supermarkets, lavender, French marigolds and, to my summer delight, yards and yards of leafy vegetables – chard, spinach, lettuce, a shelter crop that Isabel harvested in great armfuls for us to take and chomp our way through.

The garden proper at Ashington is anchored now by turrets of yew, axial paths and wide herbaceous borders, ferneries under the shade and a wild meadow coaxed back under the trees in the cider orchard. Behind the house, in the greenhouse and potting shed, Julian reigns supreme. Isabel rises at first light to compose another yard of the book she is writing, and they are both in bed by 10 p.m. Then, like a painter who discards the finished canvas for a new one, they move through the deep intimacy of creation to a sudden closure. Once comfort and serenity are established indoors and a form of perfection without, they leave, summoned away by the siren call of a glorious new creative act.

The Old Parsonage

Ben Pentreath and Charlie McCormick
2018–2024

The oldest entries in Ben Pentreath's Inspiration blogs go right back to BC – before Charlie McCormick – before Ben and Charlie met and married. 'BC' was Ben working away on the sloping land behind the Old Parsonage every weekend, growing roses and a couple of beds of dahlias, the rest mostly under grass. But Charlie was a born farmer and a grower, lately working for Bridget Elworthy of the Land Gardeners at Wardington Manor (see page 137). Thanks to his restless innovation, these acres rioted each summer and took every prize at local agricultural shows with all kinds of vegetable and ever-changing herbaceous borders that grew 2 metres (6 feet) high in July and August. There were dogs, chickens and, just beyond the garden walls, the quiet graveyard beds of the little grey estate church where Charlie's flowers migrated to vases set on the stone window-sills when it was his Sunday on the flower rota.

Massed together like a field of barley, foxglove, love-in-a-mist, angelica and lady's mantle shouldered upwards, shrub roses and antlered cardoons pushed up in between. Garden chairs stood around at companionable angles coloured in glossy Pantone colour-chart blue or orange. Spidery-armed pelargoniums filled upstairs window-sills, and dahlia season was legendary, Charlie's polychromed crops gathered and given to lucky friends by the bucketful. Charlie won medals and prizes for onions, flowers, marmalade, marrows, roses! Eventually, he judged these classes at the local Melplash agricultural show too. The *hortus conclusus* of the parsonage had never been so abundantly planted, so bountifully productive. But Charlie is a native New Zealander by way of Scotland and so the craving for larger acres, wider boundaries and fewer fences has carried them both on and away, to pastures new.

PREMIER BLOOM

CHARLIE MCCORMICK
JUDGE
THE ROSE SOCIETY UK

HORTUS
GARDENING IN BRITAIN
HORTUS
Dorset
A SHELL GUIDE
by Michael Pitt-Rivers
BRICKS and FLOWERS

Belinda Eade

Shropshire and Somerset

2022

For almost all of the long time I have known her, Belinda Eade has carved stone and built grottoes. I have watched her arts and craft evolve with huge admiration, coveting her limpet-shell sconces owned by my friend the gardener-historian Todd Longstaffe-Gowan, the dog grave markers carved for her mother and father, her oaken panels conjuring Arcady in the King's garden at Highgrove. The shell and twig houses she made with her husband, Patrick, in Somerset are extraordinary, vigorous and robust, as is the walled kitchen garden framed out of scrap bricks, wood, corrugated iron and found materials.

When Belinda was taking leave of the Welsh borders house in which she and her siblings grew up, I stayed a night and spent a Proustian day among the half-emptied potting sheds and glasshouses, the sub-basements full of thriftly stored-away apple boxes, wellingtons and waterproofs. Outhouses, woodsheds, mounded artichoke beds and mossed-over paths testified to a century of heavy, determined garden labour, now fallen into abeyance and ended. This was the nursery in which Belinda had learned how to plant and grow and make and extend her own domain from the nondescript overgrown state in which she found it to a marvellous terrain, fostering and settled around her old house on its hilltop site. I found these triste, abandoned glasshouses, with ferneries sprouting through earth floors and cobwebs thickening the window panes, more beautiful than any others in full fig and tidy plenitude.

Jasper Appleby-Sherring

Camberwell, London

2022

When Jasper Appleby-Sherring left art school, his degree show was a series of vegetable paintings and coiled terracotta pots planted with kale and wild grasses. A year afterwards he was training at the Chelsea Physic Garden and doubling up at weekends on the Camberwell allotment plot that had been his mother's. Most things growing there are vegetables, more kale and the spectacular loofa featuring in another painting that became a birthday present of mine. The allotment became the setting for a tiny Chateau Orlando photoshoot with Luke Edward Hall, Jasper kindly posing in various jumpers from Luke's first knitwear collection, Luke snapping with a £5 disposable camera. I took some more photos for the first issue of *The Bible of British Taste* magazine, and between us we bought his degree-show paintings, four studies of bolted flowering chard. Jasper is the assistant gardener at Osterley Park, in London, now.

Avenue House

Todd Longstaffe-Gowan
2016–2022

I met Todd Longstaffe-Gowan when we were both quite young. He was extraordinarily handsome, with a drawly Canadian accent, and already a rising garden historian and designer. But in the small square beds of communal gardens behind their Dartmouth Park flat, his partner Tim Knox was gardening and planting standard roses for their hilarious names such as 'Disco Dancer' and 'Barbara Cartland'. I remember Tim pointing them out at a long-ago summer garden party, for they were flamboyant versions of the standard tea roses beloved of my parents in the front and back gardens of my childhood home. Todd often gardens in far-flung places, but early one morning I caught a train to Malvern and watched him build a spectacular thatched fowl house in the style of Humphry Repton for their annual spring show. The judges gave it first prize, inventing a brand new category to accommodate its brilliant weirdness – with bantams picking their way among ruins and old-fashioned shrub roses – it was the show's star attraction that year.

Then Todd and Tim moved to the provinces, a huge shaggy garden that was almost a park – and its capacious Regency glasshouse that was part ruined and rotting. Todd does nothing in the ordinary and so has the patience and skill to mend something like that, not just its old glass and joinery but also elements of reinvention – for half buried at one end were the remains of a tiny grotto and fernery among broken panes and shattered shards of the handmade stalactites that had festooned it. Old glass was sourced in Poland, fine glazing bars carefully remade and stalactites modelled and cast in plaster and wire. Todd devised a drip-feed system of copper irrigation pipes, coaxed rare ferns and mosses into vigorous life and resurrected the goldfish pool with a golden toad jetting a tiny fountain spout from between fleshy lips. The wooden amphitheatre staging in the main room carries cacti, succulents and pelargoniums, all things that can flourish and look after themselves without too much heat or water.

Sir Roy Strong

Ledbury, Hertfordshire
2023

Sir Roy Strong designed Sir Elton John's first grown-up flower garden and he is constantly reinventing and renewing his own. As a noted garden historian he knows all about historical planting styles but chooses to play with and subvert the conceits he adopts from past ages. He is very good at building things, petits triannons and tiny temples, paths and garden rooms, terracing and bastion walls. Statues and obelisks are very much his thing, and he is not at all averse to a bit of new Haddonstone or Roman cement when Coade, marble or lead are out of reach. Plants are there for memory or meaning, for scent and prettiness or to complement the hard surfaces.

The Laskett in Herefordshire was Roy's masterpiece, coming into its first fruition with his wife, the theatre designer Julia Trevelyan Oman, then given a fresh chop and restyle during the years after her death in 2003. The smaller town garden behind his red brick regency villa in Ledbury is an old and new combo, its new-built curtain walls already sweetened with roses, delphiniums, lupins and rosemary bushes, and all reigned over by the pumped-up, larger-than-life statue of the god Pan, hairy goat pelt and muscly arms folded and ready for business. From his Arcadia in a foamy sea of herbaceous perennials, Pan leers across at a coy straw-hatted Rococo-era gardener's boy, hand on hip, resting on his spade. They are definitely 'in conversation'.

Bettiscombe Manor

Jasper Conran

2022

Jasper Conran and his husband, Oisin, live in one of the most settled places that I know (see also page 144). The house is old, a seventeenth-century farm and manor that had been a yeoman dwelling for centuries, its panelled walls and outbuildings staying unaltered but burnished by everyday use. House and garden are silted down on their gently sloping site to look out across a wide undulating landscape of greenness, with fields and dew ponds buffering the slopes beyond its low enclosing walls. When I was last there, summer was going out and autumn coming in; the beds in the potager and kitchen garden were full and heavy with collapsing sunflowers and dahlias, Michaelmas daisies and gladioli; the pea sticks and artichokes were toppling back to earth; lettuces and cabbages were getting ready to bolt; and tomato plants were bowing under the weight of their fruits. It's a picking garden and an eating garden, with fat hens a-laying and greenhouses full of chilli peppers, herbs, pelargoniums and vegetable seedlings coming on. And it's a cutting and looking-at garden: 'Tulips, irises, roses, dahlias – that is roughly how my year breaks down,' Jasper says.

Sean Anthony Pritchard

Mendipp Hills, Somerset

2024

Sean Anthony Pritchard's cottage floats in its cottage garden, islanded between two country lanes, set back on the thick end of its long, triangulated site. Garden verdure runs up to its gloss-green front door. In July everything is bowing over, crashing and splurging over the paths after drenching rain, flower heads seeding and dropping. But there are roses and nasturtiums outside and in, intense hot orange flowers in bowls and little cups, fat roses clustered in a spectrum of pinks and that dirty yellow of old sateen bedspreads.

This was a farm labourer's dwelling, built at the end of the seventeenth century, low-ceiled, with thick stone walls. Bedrooms and kitchen were added or extended afterwards, the floors and walls know nothing of the plumb line. And so every picture hangs a little askew, tabletops are tip-tilted, candlesticks and table lamps stagger slightly like drunks leaving the pub at closing time. The rooms inside are stages for the flowers and plants in Sean's garden, grandstanded on piles of books or magazines, balanced on the cane seat of a wobbly chair, in jugs and pots and dishes and buckets. Sean thinks of himself as the curator of his own house-museum, everything chosen and added to his rooms piquing his interest or serving the vocation he loves.

Sean is a plantsman and the book that he published in 2024, *Outside In: A Year of Growing and Displaying*, is a kind of DIY manual for what flowers when, how you might grow them and what you might do with them thereafter. It's full of his excellent photographs of cottage-dwelling life through a calendar year. The flowers are its stars, and after that the swelling gallery of flower pictures that he has amassed, growing across every inch of the walls. I was rather proud that the largest and boldest – a curiously post-Cubist rendering of a pot of scarlet geraniums – was the one he had bought from me at last December's Interiors Boot Sale, and that I had found at the very end of a trawl around the Rosudgeon car boot sale and enjoyed through one winter on my own kitchen wall. I liked it much more in its new setting. While I took the last of these photos Sean was in repose, leaning out against the doorpost and contemplating the garden that he had made, like God the Father on the Sixth Day of Creation.

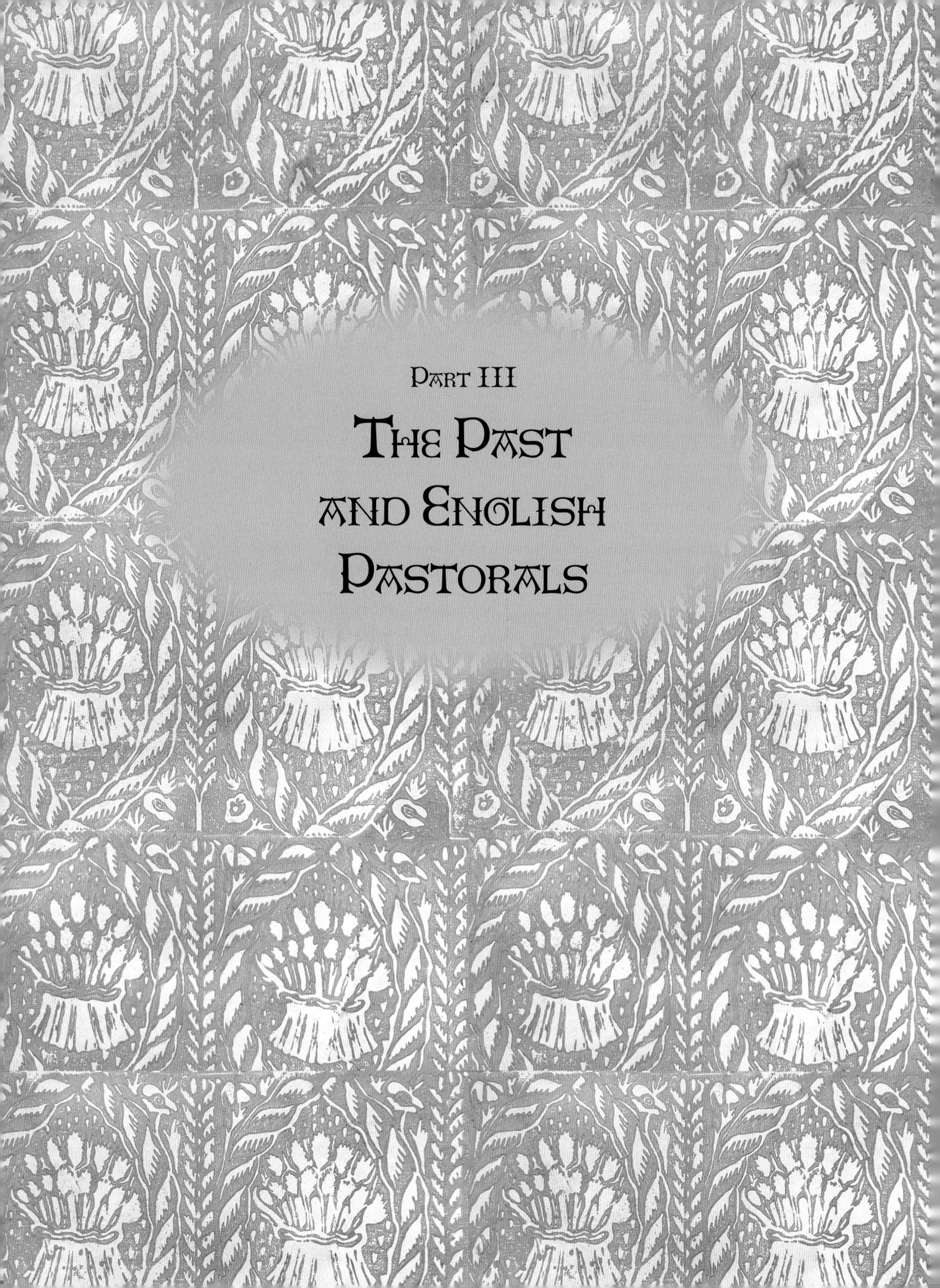

Part III

The Past and English Pastorals

GOOD OLD BRANDS

'HP Sauce improves all meals', its manufacturers promised in the 1950s. HP has been around for more than a century now, with its royal warrant and distinctive blue label featuring Big Ben and the Houses of Parliament. Earlier adverts show the bottle in a table-scape feast with lobster, chicken, ham and what looks like half a salmon; I was more conservative as a child and consumed it in plain brown-bread sandwiches. When Bridie Hall (see page 111) and I were conjuring up a pop-up shop with the theme of 'London' I stipulated that there must be sauce bottles, and Bridie made me very proud with a beautiful mantle-scape tribute honouring good-old HP.

In the 1970s, when central heating was rare, the two-bar electric fire got us out of bed on winter mornings. One side of your body roasted in searing incandescent heat that could easily melt and fuse the fabric of a Bri-Nylon nighty. There's a green one in Virginia Woolf's bedroom at Monk's House in Sussex, and lots more to be seen in photographs of the late Queen relaxing at home. Alan Bennett has one that I covet with sort of Georgian curlicues done in 1940s' chrome. Useful and especially nice looking, I think these old fangled inventions are completely indispensable.

At a certain point around 20 years ago, I started saving white plastic Fairy Liquid bottles, troubled by Procter & Gamble's laissez faire attitude to the classic space-rocket cylindrical design. For a while I was decanting the emerald-green liquid from new squeezy bottles into one of my old ones, then I thought it too ridiculous and stopped. Wanting to dispose of my hoarded bottles, I found that I was not alone – there was a strong resale market on eBay and various friends were thrilled when I passed mine on to them. Then the new 'hipped' transparent bottle design was gone as well, and the bottles acquired an ugly flash on the label and dwindled in size. Now they've been turned upside down, like cheap sauce bottles, and I'm regretting my impulsive generosity.

THE DANCING ENGLISH
THE ENGLISH
FOLK DANCE & SONG SOCIETY

Folklore and Mythologies

Years ago I saw a ladies Morris hand dancing gravidly at the Royal Cornwall Show. Morris wasn't a 'thing' back then, and nor were: 'folk culture'; paganism, standing stones and holy wells; agricultural shows and allotments; folk music, knitting and mending; corn dollies; old-school tattoos; real ale; traditional crafts; giant vegetables; back-yard chickens; prize dahlias; white witches and hedge witches; microdosing; lurchers and whippets; artisan foods and expensive artisan clothing; nor all the other nonsensical, wonderful or serious pursuits and fetishes that many of us are rather enjoying just now.

When things like these move up from niche to television shows and Saturday supplements, you have to pay attention. Folk happens in the landscape (so says the author Alan Garner) and the landscape is a curtain behind which memories and ancient legends live and evolve. William Wordsworth and his daffodils, Joni Mitchell singing 'We've got to get ourselves back to the garden' at Woodstock in 1970 – myths of pastoral, nature and the seasons turning hold eternal truths that continue to pull us in.

Morris Renascent

The Morris is where I came in as an awe-struck child and now Morris is having a beautiful revival. Half a dozen Christmases ago, looking for something to do in the doldrums of Boxing Day, I persuaded my Oxfordshire sisters and their broods to come and watch their local hand – The Eynsham Morris – dancing around the half a dozen pubs in their eponymous village, and we were not disappointed. The Eynsham Morris is a glorious, lively and very local troop straddling youth and age with strong legs and voices, and the most beautifully crafted outfits, and they jump high into the air like crickets, dancing for pure joy. The fellowship between dancers and onlookers is palpable; that the Morris is customarily performed within the purlieus and communality of a public house is equally crucial.

Then in 2019, in the pre-dawn darkness of an Oxford Mayday morning, Emma Bridgewater took me to see them again, bringing in the spring, dragging the Oxford Ox over the bridge from Port Meadow with a naked maiden riding on its back, the very final performance of this heart-stopping ritual and one that I will never forget. Two years ago we sought and found Boss Morris on another May Day dawning on the cowslip-meadowy commons outside Stroud, dancing as new-minted and glorious as Botticelli's Venus rising fresh from the waves. Old folk and new folk, Boss Morris is boss of them all.

Welcome to
WALTON-ON-THE-
SMASHING
SWIRL
Male Voice Choir
Remember the Poor
1724
ST. BURYAN
VINTAGE RALLY
DA FEELGOOD!
MUMMY
PLAYER'S
PLAYER'S
NAVY CUT
SWEENEY TODD'S
Fishing Bait
Bag it with
Mag-it
8

BUTCHER
WINDSOR ESTD 1780
ALL CATTLE from the ROYAL ESTATES
ELECTRIC
EXPERT
JUST A LINE FROM HERNE
Henry RIP Hicks
SUN RISEN
BASC
BASC
Buy your fresh
POLDARK EGGS
'Ere!
EGGS
FRESH
£1·20
½ Dozen
Providing more
space for psychological
distancing
Camden
3

Oh, do not tell the priest our plight,
Or he would call it a sin;
But – we have been out in the woods all night,
A-conjuring Summer in!

– *A Tree Song* by Rudyard Kipling

Back to the Garden

Once you start looking out for the folk customs and traditions of the past, once you have tied a ribbon on a bough overhanging a holy well, ascended to Glastonbury Tor or trodden a sheep-track though the grass looping a stone circle, the desire for a more total immersion can be hard to resist. Every year the spectacle of white-robed druids ascending the tarmacked path to the top of Primrose Hill stops the traffic at solstice or equinox. It is a curiously innocent event rounded off with a picnic and trip to the pub, although I've never been attracted since finding out that one of their number is my husband's dentist. But the old magic comes in many guises.

Near Land's End, where I have spent a bit of time, there are quite a lot of witches about. At a low ebb one winter, I was about to consult the St Buryan village dark witches but was warned off them by a learned green, or hedge, witch I met at a drinks party in Penzance's Morrab Library. I had just noticed that my birthday fell on Walpurgis Night, or Witches' Night – or rather, was one day out, but apparently that still qualified me as one of 'them' in parts of eastern Europe. Enchantingly, my daughter's painter friend was 'Hot Disney Witch' on Instagram but changed this to align her name more closely with her vocation. Then I spent some time with Simon Costin – long of the Craft and keeper of the Museum of Magic and Witchcraft and the Museum of British Folklore – and Steve Patterson, devisor of Falmouth's Museum of Magic and Folklore – and realised that I was out of my depth.

Re-enchanted Lands and 'Real' Folk

Now that folk is thoroughly 'cool' and our appetite for all these things keeps on growing, there have been accusations of ethnocentricity, tussles over ownership and retellings of history, the cultural appropriation of heritage that was once the fairly exclusive domain of quite 'other' people. Nevertheless, when I was imagining this book I knew I wanted to bring in pastoral, mythologies, neopaganism and standing stones, folklore and folk culture, church kneelers, painted fairground horses and flower and agricultural shows, while remaining a bystander and an amateur, not a player. Myth takes us into a place of time travel, recurring patterns and multiple realities that produce their own truths.

When I was younger I had a thing about Herne the Hunter and the Wild Hunt, my imagination and night terrors fed by the manifestations in John Masefield's book *The Box of Delights* (1935) and anything written by Alan Garner. In the West Country we have spent a lot of time poring over large-scale OS maps looking for standing stones that were off the beaten track, mapped by eighteenth-century antiquarians and photographed for John Michell's brilliant acid-trip-inspired book, *The Old Stones of Land's End* (1974).

These things bring a magical dimension to the quotidian, for this region at the Land's End is both a 're-enchanted land' – with its seekers in Lamorna Valley questing for the ghost of Ithell Colquhoun and pagan hand-fastings in the Merry Maidens stone circle – and a place where 'trad folk' (or real folk) is still going on everywhere, all the time. During lockdown I worshipped one majestic menhir that stands sentinel on my farmer friends' pastures, since the village church and its services were denied to us. In 2012 I had photographed the wool-work kneelers in that church – extraordinary, personal works of art and craft that became one of the bibleofbritishtaste's first-ever blog posts – and took to seeking out their original begetter and stitcher Sheila Hosking after Matins. I had hung about on the farm too, photographing the complicated choreography of 7 a.m. milking and drawing out anecdotes of 'Feyther' and the pretty names given to the 74 milch cows whose grandchildren and great-grandchildren still grazed fields mapped in the Domesday Book. There was Morvah Pasty Day (the remains of a Lammas fair associated with the local legend of Jack the Tinkard), when the pasties always ran out, enthusiasts inhaling the cindery fumes at Stithians Steam Rally and the local Memorial Agricultural Rally, when Garfield Gilbert drove his ancient Massey Ferguson around the show ring as if it were a charger on the battlefield of Agincourt, to the cheers and jeers of the folk he had once lorded it over at school. There is still (just) the beautiful tradition called 'Crying the Neck' when the last handful of barley corn is ceremonially cut at harvest's end, and the Spring Flower Show in Marazion, full of exquisite early narcissi and camellias, where I once photographed the funniest vegetable sculpture ever.

Google mapped them all (and so did I). There's a tsunami of new 'folky' stuff out there now, satisfying our eternal atavistic ache for anything that takes us 'back to nature', for these things warm us and bind us together. My friend Lally Macbeth is doing a brilliant job of proselytising for old folk and new with The Folk Archive and her ingenious creation Stone Club; I can't fault her taste as it chimes so closely with my own. On the farm, driven by historically low profit margins, Deryck and David Eddy have given up milking and gone over to beef, but the fields still bear their eternally ancient names. I think it's time to put away my camera and 'get back to the garden', as Joni Mitchell sang so presciently. Their tallest standing stone and I still have things to say to each other.

PENDEEN
COVE
2 MILES
MORVAH
2 MILES
SANDER
NAILS
CREWKERNE
FOLK
DANCE
GROUP
VINTAGE VEHICLE
St BURYAN
RALLY
FAMILY DOG SHOW SATURDAY 2 O'CLOCK
SATURDAY
SUNDAY
JULY
30
31
OPEN 10 AM
LIVE MUSIC
SATURDAY 9PM
MADRON
O.C.S.
MADRON
O.C.S.

Duncan Harvey

Flower farmer, West Penrith

This is Duncan Harvey, a flower farmer who still grows and sells flowers from a few fields at Land's End, near the house in which he was born. The work is seasonal and on a tiny scale, his flowers – early narcissus, old-species daffodils, violets and pinks, are bunched and sold within two or three miles of the ground in which they spring up. There are few like him, for this is a subsistence living that was eked out between potato rows and farm husbandry or fishing, back in the day and according to the turning of the year. Violets and narcissus are for winter and early spring; then pinks, irises and sweet williams serve for Valentine's Day, Mothering Sunday and for the buttonholes of mourners at funerals. It has become a labour of love and of habit now, more or less, he explained, while bunching flowers for the weekly church market and for his roadside stall.

My father done violets, I remember picking violets when I was in primary school bunchin 'em. We had the meadows up home, down cove, before rabbits come back again, that was.

A lot of people did around here, the ones that was doing fishing, were doing violets, a lot of the fishermen – if they had a little bit of ground – they'd grow some early potatoes or grow a piece of violets just to fill in and get them through the winter when the weather was . . . After that they'd switch off. We used to send them off to all the markets, a lot up to Nottingham – George Smalley up in Nottingham, Birmingham, in the 70s.

My father was working with my grandfather on the farm and then it was something extra, that was it. My dad passed away when he was 58, around '88, so he finished quite young, so I finished with the cattle, then I was doing the flowers on top – we was milking a small herd up there. I gave up the farm and just kept the land down here. I was mostly full time on flowers anyway, I liked the calves side of it more than the milking side. So there haven't been any cows up there, Boscean, since then.

This one is Sir Winston Churchill, they'll be in for Mother's Day. This one's called Early Bride, that is a nice one. These ones are called Valentine 'cos they generally come in around the Valentine's time. We used to send them off to all the markets. We sent violets off to a big funeral up in Birmingham – they wanted 15 boxes – for one funeral! – that would have been 900 bunches?

My mother likes the flowers, she likes some daffs. I think she's seen enough of the violets. Do you want to look at the violets on the way out? They're not very big plants, one time you could have them as big as a dinner plate or could do. The deer got most of them, they're coming to the end now.

WHY THE PUB IS MY HOME FROM HOME

We never went to pubs when I was a child. My mother came from a farming background that she didn't care to acknowledge; as a schoolchild she had been taken on visits to country kinsfolk who were not genteel. An element of drinking was involved but never fully spelt out. And so we were given to understand that pubs were horrid places, to be avoided.

The only exception was on Boxing Day morning in our Surrey village, a small place with a railway station that fed commuters into London. Watching from our front windows, one of my sisters would give a shriek: 'Quick! Half-a-horse is going past!' And we were off, bundling into outdoor clothes and following behind to see the Thames Valley Morris Men dancing on their annual fixture around the five village pubs. We usually went to stand outside the largest, nearest and soberest, The Foley Arms. This was the 1960s. The beardy Thames-men danced very methodically, clashing swords and wafting handkerchiefs, some lifting elderly knees from the tarmac with difficulty. To five-year-old me, they seemed God-like creatures, but one or two were easily as old as the century, keeping up the camaraderie of their wartime service. Half-a-horse bobbed and wove among them, pulling the string that chattered his hobby-horse's wooden

jaws. Now I know that this was Cyril Smith, bagman and founder of this Morris hand in 1952, ex Home Guard, trade unionist, librarian and Justice of the Peace. The fact that one or two of his comperes had been in church on Remembrance Sunday and another officiated at the local flower show sanctioned our presence at this pagan revel. We were never bought crisps or anything fizzy to drink, yet for me this much anticipated novelty became the most thrilling day of the year, surpassing even Christmas.

Crossing the Threshold

I've kept my fondness for the Morris, but pubs were bound to be catnip to me after this. Between the ages of 15 and 16 I became a regular at The Foley Arms with my friend Marianne, worldlier and more daring than me. We had pineapple-flavoured lip gloss for sophistication and Sobranie Menthol cigarettes. We went there illicitly on Sunday evenings, keeping low behind the pub garden's privet hedge when we were supposed to be attending the Youth Fellowship's guitar and worship meetings. No one ever reported on us or paid us any attention at all.

As soon as I left school, during the extended interval between A-level exams and results, I got a job as a barmaid. The pub in question was on our village cricket green, popular and a bit raffish. I served large G & Ts to balding men in leather blousons and Wrangler jeans who drove up in Triumph Stags and Lotuses and threw their car keys and packets of Silk Cut onto the bar. Shallow cut-glass ashtrays the size of fruit bowls stood all along the bar counter and at closing time I sluiced them in boiling water, liquid nicotine running in rivulets down my bare arms. I got chatted up, fell for an alcoholic university drop-out who propped up the bar every night and left, love-sick and regretful, as the autumn term came around.

'Only connect!' says E.M. Forster's Margaret Wilcox in the novel *Howards End* (1910). Some find connection in a church congregation or the safety of family, book clubs or beloved pets, but for so many others – the lonely, unlovely, bonhomous or boring – the pub is their home from home. I count myself among them, for to be welcomed in or even just tacitly accepted in a pub bar is the most warming experience I know. In the middle of my life I'm always scouting for this kind of unsmart, 'wet' pub, somewhere that's becoming harder and harder to find. I've perfected the art of the 'cold' entry into a traditional public bar by sending our inexpensive-looking old lurcher in first at the end of her lead. The regulars on the bar stools first look down, then up, and by the time we're at the bar a bit of dog chat oils our arrival.

The Winner, lost

But just like old friendships, cherished pubs can go wrong on you or end suddenly. One profound sorrow of mine concerns the obscure little pub in the village where I grew up known as The Winner or Winning Horse. My mother's snobbish intolerance for this modest place had piqued my childish curiosity when we had passed it on walks with our dog, and so, tidying her grave in the sheeting rain one day, I decided to try it.

Run by the same family for over 70 years, The Winner was indisputably and exclusively local, with off-sales and a little glass display cabinet holding sweeties and cigarettes in its porch. There were two or three men in high-viz lunching on lager and crisps

in the dark Public Bar, ancient linoleum and a coke fire in the minute grate. The dog went in front of me and when they had finished with her it was my turn to explain my origins to the curious barmaid of about my own age. Warming to me and keen to establish our common ground, her regulars easily blew my cover with a direct question about which of the village primary schools I had attended. 'My mother was the dinner lady there,' said the barmaid into the flat silence that fell when I named the fee-paying one. Now, with hindsight, I see how my 50-odd years of connection to this village have been meted out inside its several not very nice or particularly special pubs and how each – and this one last of all – has served in its different way to house or console.

Then suddenly, in 2019 I found The Winner closed and boarded up. 'Thank you for your trade and friendship' said a scrap of paper written in felt-tip and stuck inside the window; and there was another hole torn in the frayed social fabric of this dim little place that won't easily be mended.

There is nothing to
put in the place of
BEER
a necessity to the
Strength of Britain
"We've won on Beer before;
We'll win with Beer again."

BELL INN
Award Winning
Real Ales

The Female Experience

Which brings me to the subject of women in pubs, one as mixed as the experience of female emancipation itself. As with so many other prejudices, misogyny will always exist, for like many good things, pubs were, in the main, designed for men. For my part I observe the unspoken protocols, exchange my pleasantries at the bar, then sink down gratefully in a corner.

I am still searching for the Babycham advertisement that I think I saw years ago exhorting husbands not to leave their wives at home, to bring them along to the pub and ply them with this sweet, low-alcohol fizzy drink so that at closing time they could take the wheel and pilot their husbands home again, safe from the danger of a breathalyser. But I haven't been able to track it down, so this Babycham beermat dating from about a decade later, must do service in its place.

INDEX

ACKNOWLEDGEMENTS

Thank you, so much, to all the owners of all the houses and gardens, all the Morris hands – and Cornish flower farmer Duncan Harvey – who allowed me to take their photographs and reproduce them in this book. To my talented book designer Jack Henshall who designed and laid out its pages again and again, and to Laura Bulbeck, Anna Watson and Isabel Eeles who edited and skilfully steered it into port. And to Sophie Scard at United Agents, who found me its publisher.

Emma Hardy of Sanderson Design Group gave me hours of help in their archive. Marthe Armitage and her daughter Jo Broadhurst gave me her lovely Gardeners wallpaper for my endpapers, Blithfield and Co., Jane Hill and Emma Gibson helped with Peggy Angus's Cornstooks wallpaper. Erica Fairfax-Lucy allowed me to put Charlecote on the cover. Benedict Foley and Daniel Slowik of Nuthall Temple gave me their classy Ivy Trellis for page114. Bride Hall styled the HP Sauce bottle picture used in Good Old Brands back in 2013, and comes to the pub with me on Fridays.

Charlie Hopkinson, Katie Fontana, Dan Cruickshank, Derry Moore and Richard Hewlings helped with photos for the Spitalfields chapter, Laurence Llewelyn-Bowen and Marthe Armitage helped with dear old William Morris, Caroline Roberts took the pictures of Virginia Woolf's 'Room of One's Own' in the Bloomsbury chapter. Simon Mills, Ben Pentreath, Jasper Conran and Mark Hearld lent me some of their own photos too. Louise Guinness came up trumps and drove me to Biddesden, where Rosaleen Mulji, Catriona, Fiona and Finn Guinness were so kind and accommodating. Jane Hill helped with Bloomsbury references and Nathaniel Hepburn gave me a glorious day alone at Charleston Farmhouse, with Kathy Crisp, who knows everything.

More thanks to my dear friend Ben Pentreath, who read the text at an early stage and was so nice about it. And to another dear friend Luke Edward Hall, for his Foreword, helping with designs in last minute emergencies and for always being so encouraging. To Rupert Thomas, once my generous editor at *The World of Interiors*, where this all began. To dearest Georgie Wilson and Andrew Wilson who are sometimes there when photographs are being taken or tar barrels are flaming, and my mother and father, who are dead, but not forgotten.

Quarto

First published in 2025 by Frances Lincoln,
an imprint of The Quarto Group.
One Triptych Place, London, SE1 9SH,
United Kingdom
T (0)20 7700 9000
www.Quarto.com

EEA Representation, WTS Tax d.o.o.,
Žanova ulica 3, 4000 Kranj, Slovenia
www.wts-tax.si

A catalogue record for this book is available from the British Library.

ISBN 978-0-7112-9401-1
Ebook ISBN 978-0-7112-9402-8

10 9 8 7 6 5 4 3 2

Design by Jack Henshall

Publisher Philip Cooper
Commissioned by Anna Watson
Senior Editor Laura Bulbeck
Senior Designer Isabel Eeles
Senior Production Controller Rohana Yusof

Printed in Huizhou, Guangdong, China TT112025

PICTURE CREDITS

Endpapers, and p.8 background: Gardeners – Hand Printed Wallpaper from Marthe Armitage Prints - Original design by Marthe Armitage

p.14: Very Diana Rigg, very Sanderson, advertisement *c.* 1973–75, copyright Sanderson Design Group

pp.15, 18: William Morris, Wallpaper printing logbook, Jeffrey and C. for Morris & Co., *c.* 1875–1927, Daisy p.15 and Trellis p18 bottom, both 3 colourways; copyright Sanderson Design Group

p.17 left: Kennet, 1883, William Morris, Birmingham Museums Trust/ Birmingham Museum and Art Gallery

p.18 top: Kelmscott House Hammersmith by Emery Walker, copyright William Morris Gallery, London Borough of Waltham Forest

p.19: Old Man's Beard – Hand Printed Wallpaper from Marthe Armitage Prints – Original design by Marthe Armitage

p.20: Our man introduced the English Country Cottage Look, advertisement, *c.* 1966–97, copyright Sanderson Design Group

p.21: Brer Rabbit, printed textile, William Morris, Philadelphia Museum of Art (public domain)

pp.23, 24: Monks House, Rodmell, Sussex, copyright Caroline Roberts

p.30: Spitalfields, 1970s, copyright Dan Cruickshank

p.32 top: copyright Derry Moore, taken for *The Englishman's Room*, Alvilde Lees-Milne and Derry Moore, 1986

pp.33–36: copyright Plain English Design

p.37 top & bottom: Spitalfields, copyright Charlie Hopkinson

p.73 top & bottom: copyright Ben Pentreath

p.146 bottom right: copyright Jasper Conran

pp.238–39: Cornstooks, hand printed wallpaper by Peggy Angus, copyright estate of Peggy Angus

p.247, bottom row, images 1 and 3: copyright Mark Hearld